HOW TO GIVE AWAY YOUR *LIFE*

by

Paul E. Little

[redacted]

HOW TO GIVE AWAY YOUR *LIFE*

By Paul E. Little

Scripture quotations in this book are from the Revised Standard Version of the Bible, except where otherwise noted.

Library of Congress Catalog Card No. 78-71261

ISBN 0-88449-063-7

Printed in the United States of America.

CONTENTS

Contents

FOREWORD

God has brought me in touch with certain men of outstanding talent. One such was my friend the late Paul Little whom I first came to appreciate in a special way in 1957 when he tirelessly reached out to university students in our 16-week New York Crusade. I have deeply admired him as a man of God, with extraordinary insights into the work of God and boundless enthusiasm for communicating the Word of God.

I sense a great personal loss because Paul is no longer with us and feel privileged to recommend this stimulating series of talks which he gave at The Village Church I once pastored in suburban Chicago.

In his unique way Paul describes "the electricity of Christ's claim" that He is the solution to the "moral power-failure" of our time. Then he shows how Jesus Christ says to us today as clearly as He did to the thief on the cross, "You, too, can be with me in Paradise."

Maybe you have stood on the perimeter of Christianity and questioned what it is all about. Is it really true? Does it have any pertinence to my life? What happens if I ignore it? Or perhaps you have been discouraged in the past by some ponderous, cliche'-ridden explanations. This book, then, is for you. You will find here an authenticity that comes from a man unconditionally devoted to Jesus Christ Himself.

PREFACE

A couple of friends had come to our home for dinner. The roast beef was finished and it was time to clear the table, bring on the coffee, and serve the dessert. As usual, when kindred minds and sharp wits were gathered together in our home, the author of this book, my husband, would be at his fascinating best. One guest brought a stack of dirty dishes into the kitchen and asked apologetically, "Do you need my help? The conversation is so exciting, I don't want to miss one word that Paul is saying!"

It was this kind of sparkle that made it fun to be with Paul and made his lectures and messages come alive. Like anyone else, he had his average moments, too, (like glumly taking out the garbage) but when he was inspired, he came through with a wallop!

In reality, this book had been on the drawing board for some time. Paul's files contained a section marked "Books to be Written," and one folder was labeled "The Christian Life." In it he had listed his projected chapter titles which I have used as an approximate guide in organizing these materials. Thanks to our electronic age, the entire contents of the book has been taken from taped lectures given to audiences in a variety of places ranging from student retreats to church conferences.

Chapter One was known affectionately in our home as THE parable. When Paul said he was going to preach on THE parable we knew which one, because for him there was only one. It had encouraged many Christians so he repeated it to new audiences without apology. Chapter Two was published in abridged form in *Moody Monthly* Magazine only one month before his fatal automobile accident in 1975. It bore the prophetic title, "The God Who Never Lets Things Just Happen."

To transcribe Paul's spoken word into written form and still retain the view through Paul-colored glasses was not always easy. The dynamism of his voice and personal passion could give an explosive element to a simple sentence like, "Service in God's vineyard carries in itself its own great reward. I'm so thankful that I'm in His vineyard!" This element does not readily transfer onto the written page. Undoubtedly, those who knew him will unconsciously fill in this gap for themselves, although I did seek continuously to preserve the Paul-isms with which he intuitively decorated all of his thoughts. But far and above his uniqueness of communication, I endeavored to preserve clearly the underlying truths and everyday applications God had shown him. Without the kind help of Florence Pauls, David Olson, the David Paveys and the encouragement of Paul's sister, Grace Emery, the whole project may never have been completed.

While finishing the editing, a number of friends were praying with me concerning the title that would reflect the book's theme of living the Christian life. Coincidentally, I "happened" to meet a graduating senior and asked him what his options were for the future. He had two; get a job back home or go on a two year missionary team. I heard myself saying to him, "Well, you can't miss if you give your life to the Lord." With that we parted. Instantly, the title came to my mind, HOW TO GIVE AWAY YOUR *LIFE*.

This title seems totally propitious and proper since it links these pages to Paul's first best seller, HOW TO GIVE AWAY YOUR *FAITH*. It also aptly describes the dominant thread woven through each chapter as capsulized in the question asked by the Apostle Paul at the time of his conversion, "Lord, what do you want me to do?" He was ready immediately to give away his life to the Lord Jesus.

Another reason the title is fitting is that my husband, Paul, unceasingly prayed the same prayer as his namesake. He prayed for God's will in his life, not as an unwelcome obligation, but with dedicated enthusiasm. Ardently he would echo Isaac Watt's hymn, "Here, Lord, I give myself away; 'Tis all that I can do." Then he sometimes expressed that he wanted to be ushered into Heaven with his boots on, and he was. His last excursion in the Lord's service was driving to preach at a church one evening during our vacation.

Paul would have surely pointed out to me that nothing happens to the Christian apart from the providential sovereignty of God. Now a new and wonderful lesson has germinated for me during the process of recovering from the overwhelming loss and reconstructing a new life for myself. That lesson is that God is also GOOD. I cannot write this preface without telling of the daily support and love that has come from the Lord Jesus Christ Himself. He has tenderly and unfailingly upheld me through every dark moment. His promises have proven unequivocally reliable and His presence has changed chaos into peace.

During the months I've poured over this material, I've been encouraged in the Lord myself. If the same experience comes to each one who reads it, the work will have been worth preserving.

This volume is dedicated to our children Deborah and Paul Jr.

Marie H. Little

1

THE PRIVILEGE OF GIVING AWAY YOUR LIFE

A story is always a good attention-getter. An experienced public speaker knows that if his audience starts to doze he can get their eyes back into focus quickly by telling a story.

Stories convey abstract truth in concrete terms. Think of Aesop's fables. All of us remember from childhood the punch lines of these fables: "Look before you leap"; "Don't kill the goose that lays the golden egg"; "Don't cry 'Wolf! Wolf!' " They stay with us for a lifetime.

Our Lord was a profound story teller. Almost half of His teaching was in parables. He knew the impact of a good story. He used parables not only to make a point but to test the sincerity of His listeners. He wanted those who were genuinely open to learn more, and to be encouraged. He also wanted to weed out those who were merely superficial curiosity-seekers.

A Rich Young Man's Question

Jesus told His disciples a unique story about a householder with a vineyard. The story followed an encounter with a very rich young man who had asked a pressing question: "Teacher, what good deed must I do to have eternal life?" (Matthew 19:16).

Jesus's answer was straight from the second half of the decalogue. "Thou shalt not kill, steal, commit adultery or lie; honor your father and mother." Astonishingly, the young man replied, "All of these things I have kept from my youth up." Amazing fellow! He was convinced he had done pretty well. But I'd love to have met his wife or his children, his brothers or his sisters, to see if they agreed.

As you might expect, our Lord put His finger on the man's Achilles heel—as He would with any of us. "If you would be perfect," Jesus told him, "go, sell what you possess, and give to the poor." You might call this customized counseling. Our Lord saw that this particular man's big problem was money. Unless he was prepared to give himself to Jesus Christ without a single holdout, he would not truly be His disciple. There is no way to be half Christian any more than to be half married. Jesus will not share His place with anything or anyone. He asks us to give our very lives away—to Him. And such giving is a high privilege.

But that rich young man was not prepared to make Jesus Christ number one. He went away sorrowful because he had great wealth. Obviously, he didn't think Christ was worth it. He simply left.

Seeing the young man's struggle, Jesus turned to His disciples and told them how difficult it is for a rich man to enter the Kingdom of Heaven—as difficult as it is for a camel to go through the city wall's low and narrow gate that was called "the eye of a needle."

Peter's Question

By this time in the biblical event, Peter was bursting. He blurted out, "Lord, we have left everything to follow you.

We haven't turned away from you. We have forsaken *all*. What are we going to get out of it? What about our rewards?"

Nobody had to psychoanalyze Peter to find out what he was thinking. His thoughts were right on the surface. He didn't try to "snow" anybody. His question was bald and honest. And the Bible shows him in all his unvarnished reality. Like the honesty of Oliver Cromwell, who told his portrait artist to paint him the way he was, "warts and all," Peter's honesty is a great encouragement to us.

Did you ever want to ask Peter's question? Maybe you didn't verbalize it. Most of us would be afraid to. It would sound too unspiritual and materialistic. Deep down, however, that very question nags and reverberates within us. I guess we are most likely to ask it in a time of adversity, when we're feeling low.

In the middle of some tremendous difficulty the question comes up silently and agonizingly. Maybe someone in our family is having a serious health problem and we ask, "Lord, why us? We've tried to serve you with everything we have. Other people who aren't nearly so committed as we are—who perhaps make no profession for Christ at all—are disgustingly healthy." Marital problems or hassles with the children may bombard us. In agony of heart we ask, "Lord, so far as we know our own hearts, we have left everything to follow you. Why are we having to struggle like this?"

On the other hand, our Achilles heel may be financial. Jesus didn't advise every rich person he met to go sell all and give to the poor, but he left no doubt that too much concern for money is a hindrance. While we're struggling and grasping to make ends meet, other people—even people who appear altogether unconcerned about spiritual things—seem to have money coming out of their ears. On top of that, it looks as if they waste it on the most worthless things.

For the Christian student, the struggle may be academic. He may beat his brains out to come up with a C minus. At the same time a classmate who couldn't care less about genuine spirituality or winning others to Christ, just flips through the textbooks and comes out with an A.

We have these problems in our lives, and at times each of us asks, "Lord, how come? Why do I have these struggles?" It's possible we've even questioned the Lord right out loud, as Peter did.

Jesus' Encouraging Response

Our Lord's response to Peter and to us when we voice our honest feelings is encouraging. Jesus could have taunted Peter if He'd wanted to. He could have said, "Peter, that's very interesting. You've left everything to follow me? Well, now tell me, what is this everything you've left? As Peter tried to recount the "all" he had left for Christ, his ego probably would have begun to shrink. After four or five minutes he'd begin to feel like change for three cents. He'd feel like slinking away in humiliation, wondering why he'd been so foolish as to raise the question in the first place.

But that didn't happen. In the first place, Jesus knew that this was not a new Christian's question. Peter's question was a symptom of a "down-the-road-a-piece" disease in Christian living. Earlier, in the full flush of first commitment, Peter really had left all to follow the Lord. But now, after some time had elapsed, questioning had set in.

This has happened to me. When the Alumni Magazine from the Wharton School of Finance at the University of Pennsylvania arrives at my door, I find out what's happening to my former classmates and where they're currently working. Joe So-and-So has become president of Penn Mutual. Jane So-and-So is vice-president of another corporation, obviously making a bundle. And I? I was graduated in accounting, but my income now is what I would have started out making in that field twenty-five years ago.

I could easily let such comparisons distort my thinking. I've been serving the Lord for a long time now. What am I going to get out of it?

The gentleness of the Lord with Peter in his honesty tells us that we can completely level with Him, expose our honest thinking without reservation. In the first place, of course, there's no point in trying to fake Him out. He knows the very thoughts and intents of our hearts. We may be able to fool our Christian friends, but we cannot fool the Lord. He fully accepts and understands us in every circumstance.

In effect, what the Lord Jesus said to Peter was, "Look, Peter, don't worry. God is no man's debtor." Verbatim He said, "Every one who has left houses or brothers or sisters or father or mother or children or lands for my sake will receive a hundredfold, and inherit eternal life" (Matthew 19:29).

Some people believe this statement means that Jesus was promising us Christians enormous material prosperity. Sometimes it is handed out as gospel that if we serve Christ, great material blessings will roll in on us. This is an error. If it were true, think of all the people who would become "Christians" for the wrong motive. No, God knows money is not what reaches the inner heart. We've all read about miserable millionaires whose actions show frantic restlessness and worry. In contrast, the New Testament promises us everything that is necessary for life and godliness. A staggering benefit! In the proper perspective, this is worth more than all the material things in the world. And that's not just a Christian "party line." It's an existential fact.

God will not be in debt to anyone. Our Lord was assuring Peter of this. If we have given all we know of ourselves to all we know of Jesus Christ, He will continually pour His blessings upon us. Furthermore, the best is yet to come.

The Parable

All this is prelude to the parable. Jesus began with the question, "Do you want to know what rewards you will get and what the kingdom of heaven will be like? Well, I'll tell you." And here begins the story from Matthew 20:1-19, known as the parable of the laborers in the vineyard.

> The kingdom of heaven is like a land owner who operated a large vineyard. He found his workers for the vineyard by going to the marketplace where men were waiting to be hired. Five times during the day he went out to bring in workers—at six A.M., at nine A.M., at twelve noon, at three P.M., and finally at five P.M. Each time he was surprised to find people standing around doing nothing, and he hired them. Their standard excuse for idleness was always that no one had hired them. With the first ones who came, at six A.M., the land owner made an agreement that he would pay the customary day's wages—a denarius (a silver coin of the day). To the others, he just promised a fair wage.
>
> Sundown was quitting time. The land owner gave specific orders to his foreman: "Pay all the laborers the same, a day's wage. But pay the last arrivals first, then the next to the last and so on until all are paid." When those who came last received a full day's wages, the first ones hired naturally thought they would receive more. But, lo and behold, early starters and late starters, they all received the same amount—one denarius.
>
> Well, the first ones grumbled. "Those men worked only an hour. We worked through the hottest part of the day, yet you gave them as much as you paid us!"
>
> The land owner reminded them, "Friend, I am not doing you any injustice. You agreed to work for one denarius. If I want to give everyone the same, am I not free to do whatever I wish with my own money? Or are you envious of the others?"

Something about this parable has always jarred me and almost embarrassed me a little by a sense of its injustice. No matter how much I checked the Greek and looked up the cross-references, it still jarred me. Clearly, I had missed some insight that the Lord was trying to communicate.

One thing is absolutely certain; that land owner's unfairness does not represent our Lord's philosophy of labor-management relations. Imagine trying to operate a business on a basis of paying the same amount of money to workers who checked in at six, nine, twelve, three, and five! Absolute chaos! People could get killed rushing into the gate at five in the afternoon to start their day. Production would collapse and the whole business would fold. Whatever else the story means, it is not supposed to be the Christian's philosophy of business management; nor do I think we can build any theory of economics on it.

The Key to the Parable

Helmut Thielicke suggests that the parable is a coded telegram. He says the key to unlocking the code involves identifying the land owner, as the Lord Jesus Himself, the workers as Christians, and the work in the vineyard as service for Christ in His Kingdom. The ground-floor truth Christ wanted to convey was that to be in the Householder's vineyard and to be His servant is the greatest privilege in the world. No denarius or salary is necessary to make it worthwhile. The privilege of being in the vineyard carries within itself its own great reward.

Is this our view of serving in Christ's Kingdom? Do we have the unequivocal conviction that living and working in His vineyard is our first choice above all other options?

Rewards Versus Grace

Peter had lost sight of this privilege for the moment. He had forgotten the unconditional grace with which the Lord first invited him to "Come, follow Me." He was tempted to count up the crowns and rewards he had coming to him.

If one of us had been in his place, we might have said, "O.K., Lord, I taught this many Sunday school classes, handed out thousands of tracts, led fourteen and a half people to Christ, spent this many minutes in prayer, read this many chapters and memorized eight hundred and thirteen verses. Therefore I want twenty-seven and three-fourths crowns!" Consciously or unconsciously, we want to put God in our debt, bring out all the old IOU's and show Him how much He owes us.

That's not the way God operates. Our Lord pointed out to Peter (and to us) that crowns and rewards will be ours, but they will come because of the grace and generosity of God, the chief Householder. In His Kingdom, rewards are not on a time-card basis. No one will approach God and say, "O.K., God, here's my life. My good deeds outweigh my bad deeds, therefore I want salvation; I've earned it." No way. The Apostle Paul put it simply! "By grace you have been saved . . . it is the gift of God." The invitations of the Householder show this perfectly. He went out seeking laborers, and He had compassion on the idle men waiting to be hired. He knew they were wasting their talents and cared enough to go after them. He wanted them in His household. Entrance into God's Kingdom and the receiving of rewards for service are both available to us solely on the basis of his loving generosity.

It follows, then, that we Christians can never palm ourselves off as superior to anyone else. We cannot claim credit for being in the vineyard. We simply heard the invitation of the Householder and entered the vineyard. As for those who are still outside, we can tell them of the Householder and of His grace. When they accept His invitation, then we can share together the joys of living in the vineyard.

My wife and I saw this joy in a young Christian who took a trip with us to Wisconsin. He had come from the unkempt, rebellious set at the local high school known at the time as "the greasers." From a background of drug involvement, he had been completely delivered and brought into God's household a year before.

As we traveled he told us about a recent soireé back to a big rock concert during which he reverted to taking "speed" and began to "fly." From there he had gone from one trip to the next on any kind of drug he could get his hands on. Soon he was back into his old pattern of wheedling and bargaining for the next kick. After two weeks his mind cleared and his thoughts focused on the freedom he had left behind him. He told us how his thoughts turned to Christ. He knew that Jesus Christ, who had forgiven and freed him from guilt, was also One with whom he could share his fears. He was reliable and loving. And so were the circle of friends who drew Him to the Lord. It was a whole different life. And so much more worthwhile!

He took immediate steps back to Christ. I'll never forget the time of prayer we had as the three of us rode along in the car. It was a continuous round of praying and praising the Lord, much of the initiative being his. He just didn't want to stop. "I'll never want to leave the Lord again," he said, "Nothing compares to walking with Him." It was no put-on.

I wish I could have tape-recorded the freshness and spontaneity of that young man. No one had to program him into believing that it was great to be in the vineyard. He knew it already. It oozed from every pore. Now, not all of us have to go through the kind of struggles he had experienced. There's no need to try every sin around. That could be a dead-end street. But we've got to let the reality of God get into the marrow of our bones. We need the same deep experience of the supernatural power of Christ, the same spontaneous gratitude and the same unremitting love for our Saviour that that young man had.

Love Takes Over

The difference between serving God out of a sense of

duty and serving with joy like that young man who took the trip with us, is like comparing a housekeeper with a wife. A man who needs to have his housework done hires a housekeeper. He pays her exactly so many dollars a week. For that she's to do ten things a day—clean the floor, wash the windows, wash his socks, scrape the pots, and so on. If she doesn't do those ten things each day, no check. That's legalism, *quid pro quo*, this for that. Do it, you get paid. Don't do it, you don't get paid.

Then suppose that a strange metamorphosis takes place whereby the man and the woman fall in love and get married. Now, the relationship is entirely different. When the man goes to work, he no longer leaves a list of ten things to be done. His friends at work can say, "Hey, listen, Pal, you had better get back there with that list. Your house is going to be a shambles. Your wife is going to be sitting there with her feet on the coffee table watching TV and eating bon-bons. Nothing will get done; you'd better get that list out." But he smiles knowingly and says, "No, you don't understand. We don't need a list now."

As a matter of fact, his wife does *fifty* things a day with no list and no guarantee of any money at all. Why? She loves her husband. Cleaning floors and windows, washing socks—those chores don't "send" her any more now than before. But she does them for *him*, and that's what makes all the difference. She does it all for love.

Can we see that when love takes over in a relationship any attitude of drudgery and legalism is changed to joyful willingness? This is why we can say that service for the Householder in the vineyard carries within itself its own great reward.

Latecomer to the Vineyard

It is also true that this relationship of love makes a deep change in the perspective of the latecomer. Notice that the Householder gives the same welcome to each person whether he comes early or late. Remember the thief on the cross? In his dying moments the Lord Jesus welcomed him into His Kingdom. And if ever there was a latecomer, he was one!

The latecomer in this story is not to be envied, but to be pitied. It's interesting to meet people who have come to Christ late in life. You never meet one who gloats and says, "Ah, yes, young man, I've had the best of both worlds. I've been able to live my life for myself, but now, in my declining years, I've come to put my faith and trust in Christ. Isn't it wonderful that I have eternal life just as you have, but I have also been able to live my life for myself? Too bad you got sucked in early."

On the contrary, you will find the latecomer profoundly grateful that the denarius of salvation can be as real at five in the afternoon of their lives as it is at six in the morning.

I know personally two men who are latecomers to the Kingdom. Both have expressed intense remorse that they poured years of their energies down the drain on things that didn't amount to much instead of investing their lives for Jesus Christ in their youth. Their deep feelings about this are unremitting. Their situation is not to be envied. The ones who are most blessed are those who have responded to God's call into the vineyard early in life. They have been able to hit it with everything they've got for Jesus Christ.

In our day our Lord still welcomes all who will come into His Kingdom, the poor and the rich alike, the educated and the uneducated, the old and the young, the Jew and the Gentile, the multi-talented and the single-talented, any time they come He will receive them.

Burden and Heat of the Day

The burden and heat of the day about which the workers were complaining are not causes for lament, but causes for thanksgiving. Hold on, this is impossible! So it seems, because of the prevalent idea that if we are Christians and in fellowship with Christ, we'll have no difficulties. I don't know where that idea originated, but it's certainly not anywhere in the Old or New Testament.

Life has its share of tears and agony for everyone. This is the burden and heat. During the difficult times we come into an intimacy in prayer and fellowship with Jesus Christ that we would not have known otherwise. After we've come through it, we can give genuine thanks. Despite the agony and fear of such situations, we know that God has been with us. We know from our own experience that He is good and that His integrity and judgment are entirely dependable.

The Pay-Off

The parable ends with a skillful twist that brings out a point. It involves the procedure of paying the laborers. The landowner in the story could have paid the fellow who checked in at six in the morning and then sent him on his way. He could have done the same for those who started at nine, twelve, three and five. Presumably, no one would have known who was paid what. This would have been one of those instances when "what we don't know won't hurt us." It's not a very good maxim, but in this case it may have worked. Instead, the landowner deliberately reversed the order.

Just picture the scene. The people who started at five in the afternoon get their denarius first. Wow! You can hear the rumor going up the line: "Hey, there's going to be a bonus today!" They start to chip their teeth and grind their gears when the ones who checked in at three get paid. They also receive a denarius! Well, maybe the cut-off point is at noon for the raise. When the noon people still get only a denarius, blood pressures sky-rocket. By the time the nine o'clock people are given the same pay they are ready to lay strike plans. The whole place probably breaks into pandemonium.

For their first move, they moan their complaint directly to the landowner. He's ready. For some reason he singles out one man. With moving compassion he addresses that one worker. "My friend, I'm not being unjust to you." Then He goes on: "Am I not allowed to do what I choose with what belongs to me? Or do you begrudge my generosity?"

How would you or I reply to such an explanation? "Oh, of course not, Lord. It's wonderful that you're blessing the other person. Yes, that's great."

That's the right answer, all right, but is it really the way we would feel inside? It's hard to get our inward feelings to coincide with what we can say easily with our lips. We'd be likely to retort, "Lord, I've got shoulders broad enough to hold a lot more blessing than you're sending my way." We ourselves would like to decide what God ought to be doing in our lives and in others'. "Lord, I'm doing all the work and she's getting all the credit!"

Leave the Other Workers in God's Hands

Can you see the Lord's emphasis? He is saying, "Look, let me be the Householder and you be the servant." God knows the other person in a way that we will never know him. Furthermore, God knows you and me in a way that no other person could. I've sometimes found myself jumping to a conclusion about another person or saying something about someone, only to find a piece of information later that proved I was completely wrong. How very, very small I felt afterwards!

Well, the way to avoid this type of thing is not to make judgments about other people. Anyway, the Bible instructs us not to judge others. Leave the actions of other people with the Lord. It's a great way to get rid of anxiety. The Lord knows it all, and He can handle it.

Our concern must be, first of all, for the will of the Householder in our own lives and in our part in His vineyard. The Householder with His infinite wisdom and love is supremely able to lead us in the best path. We can confidently commit every dimension of our lives to Him and receive His freshness and joy.

If you've never entered into the vineyard, the beginning step is up to you. As in the parable, the Lord Jesus is now saying to you, "Why do you stand here all day?" He wants you in His vineyard. Your first step should be simply to recognize that Jesus Christ is the living Lord from Heaven, and that He voluntarily gave His life for you. His death bought forgiveness for our rebellion and paved the way for our entrance into His vineyard. He rose from the dead and is alive today. Because of this, each of us can enter a vital, close relationship with Him. First thank Him for what He has done for you, and then ask Him to come into your life as Savior and Lord. He will bring you into His household and you will have the singular privilege of giving away your life to Him and having the great reward of labor in His vineyard.

2

SOLID GROUND IN GIVING AWAY YOUR LIFE

Do you know what it is like to be swimming in the ocean — the Atlantic or the Pacific, and, as I have, to be swept off your feet in the crashing surf? You remember how it is—you're having a glorious time when all of a sudden, kerplop, a huge wave comes in and the next thing you know you're sprawling. Rather a shock, isn't it?

When we are knocked off our feet and go down into the water over our heads, panic sets in. We begin to choke. We thrash around. Sometimes we get bruised and everything is out of perspective. Only one thing really concerns us at this point: to get our breath and get back on solid ground. Life gets pretty basic at a time like this. What a great relief to get back onto solid ground and regain our footing.

Thrashing Panic

In the surf of life that very same thing happens to you and me as believers in Jesus Christ. Things are moving along nicely when suddenly we're knocked down and we find ourselves thrashing. Life gets out of perspective, distorted. We panic. We desperately need to get our feet back on solid ground again.

We may have been getting along fine until, without realizing it, our feet are swept out from under us and a situation overwhelms us. It might be one of the things we mentioned earlier in this book, or it might be others. Maybe the loss of a job or some other financial crisis. We may have experienced a new and unaccustomed failure. Or it might be a sudden health crisis that comes totally unanticipated. It could be a family problem of one kind or another, or being let down by a friend. We may find ourselves in the bitterness of betrayal. Perhaps your educational plans have blown sky-high. Or you were all set to be married, and somebody changed his or her mind. Whatever it is, something unexpected happens, and the thing we had counted on has been swept away. At a time like this we can lose perspective. We may thrash around, gasping for air.

Our only deliverance in such a situation is to get our feet on solid ground. One of the pieces of solid ground that enables us (with all believers throughout the centuries) to regain our perspective, is total and unshakable confidence in the providential sovereignty of God. This is a theme that runs throughout the whole of Scripture. It's one of the most basic, most stabilizing realities upon which we can put our feet. As we get hold of this fact, it takes us through the turbulences of life which inevitably come to us all. If you're in one of the calms just now, you know that sooner or later the turbulence will come. If you've just been through some turbulence, perhaps you can now look back on it from the perspective of a little calm. But in any case, times of turbulence are a normative experience for everyone at some time in life.

Sold Down the River

Joseph was one who knew something about this. Remember his story? He was literally sold down the river by his brothers. They got jealous of him because his father took delight in him and gave him a special coat, so they sold him down into Egypt. There Joseph was put into the house of Potiphar the captain of the King's guard. When Potiphar's wife tried to seduce Joseph, he literally gave her the empty sleeve, and for that act of righteousness he was put into prison. Later a couple of his prison mates, a baker and a butler, got a vision one night, and they asked him to explain it. Joseph replied, "I'll tell you what's going to happen next week: you're going to be back up there with Pharaoh. One of you is going to die, and the other is going to live." He told them which was which, too. And then he added, "Just do me one favor—when you get up there tell Pharaoh about me. I'm down here on a bum rap. Get me out of here." But the guys promptly forgot all about Joseph, and he languished still further.

Joseph had all the ingredients for a psychological profile card that would show "tilt." He had all the ingredients for self-pity, for bitterness. He could have hated his brothers with a passion that would have consumed him for a lifetime. Years later, when his brothers were finally brought into his presence as second in charge in the whole land of Egypt, he unmasked himself. At that moment those brothers thought, "Well, this is the end of the road."

God Meant It for Good

But you remember the tremendous statement Joseph made to them in Genesis 50:20: "You meant evil against me, but God meant it for good." It was Joseph's confidence in the providential sovereignty of God, his confidence that nobody and no situation could thwart God's sovereignty, that carried him through those disastrous circumstances. Anything less would have given him proper grounds for all kinds of self-pity and bitterness.

Then there was Abraham who was willing to sacrifice his

only son even though he didn't understand God's purpose, because he had confidence that God could even raise him from the dead if necessary.

David also knew something of what the providential sovereignty of God meant in everyday life. He had been told by Samuel that he was going to be king; yet Saul was out to get him, to kill him. David knew this, and Saul came very close to killing David on two occasions. At another time when David and his friends overtook Saul, they urged David, "Look, there he is! Kill him and take what you know is yours!" But David replied, "God forbid that I should touch the Lord's anointed." He was not willing to hurry God's schedule; he was willing to trust God's timing. Joab, at one point, said to David, "Look, if you don't want to do it, at least let me. Just one toss of the spear—and I won't miss." But David backed him off as well, because he believed God. Even though David knew he was destined to be king, he refused to take things into his own hands.

Abased and Abounding

Another man who knew something of the providential sovereignty of God as a basic theme throughout his life (as it can be for your life and mine) was Paul the apostle. His letter to the Philippians reveals some of the practical implications in his life.

You remember that Paul said, "I've learned how to be abased and I've learned how to abound." Well, Paul was not writing that letter during a grandiloquent period of his life. He was writing from a Roman prison, awaiting an uncertain sentence from a corrupt judge whose name was Nero. You might think that United States politics are corrupt, but they're nothing compared with Nero's.

This Roman prison from which Paul was writing was not one of the places where he was "abounding." It was no Holiday Inn, no Acapulco. It was a dank Roman prison. And yet, Paul was able to see the providential sovereignty of God in his life—in his past, in his present, and in his future. Beginning in Philippians 1:12 we read this: "I want you to know, brethren, that what has happened to me has really served to advance the gospel, so that it has become known throughout the whole praetorian guard and to all the rest that my imprisonment is for Christ; and most of the brethren have been made confident in the Lord because of my imprisonment, and are much more bold to speak the word of God without fear."

The Sovereignty of God

Has God withdrawn you from a period of active service for one reason or another? He knows all about the circumstances that brought about that withdrawal. It hasn't been an accident. A lot of us think the world will collapse without us. It's a shattering discovery when we come to realize that the world will go right on and the work of Jesus Christ will continue without us. If He takes us into a more private, secluded kind of situation from a public one, He may do this in order to remind us that we are to trust God and the only thing that really counts is where God wants us to be. If it's to be preaching to thousands of people as Paul did on one occasion, fine. If it's to be in a Roman prison chained to one other man, that's alright, too. The only thing that really counts is that you and I are where God wants us to be.

A poignant paragraph in Paul's letter to the Philippians shows how he viewed the outwardly adverse experience in which he found himself. Read it and see how he submitted to God's sovereign and loving purpose:

"Yes, and I shall rejoice. For I know that through your prayers and the help of the Spirit of Jesus Christ this will turn out for my deliverance, as it is my eager expectation and hope that I shall not be at all ashamed, but that with full courage, now as always, Christ will be honored in my body, whether by life or by death. For to me to live is

Christ, and to die is gain. If it is to be life in the flesh, that means fruitful labor for me. Yet which I shall choose I cannot tell. I am hard pressed between the two. My desire is to depart and be with Christ, for that is far better. But to remain in the flesh is more necessary on your account. Convinced of this, I know that I shall remain and continue with you all, for your progress and joy in the faith, so that in me you may have ample cause to glory in Christ Jesus, because of my coming to you again" (Philippians 1:19-26).

Paul's Secret of Joy

From one standpoint, Paul, when writing in this dismal situation, was able to write with tremendous joy and confidence because he had grasped the significance in his own experience of what the providential sovereignty of God was all about. In the first place, Paul saw God's providential sovereignty in his *past*. He says in verse 12, "I want you to know, brethren, that what has happened to me has really served to advance the gospel." Now when you consider what had happened to Paul in the past, that's a phenomenal statement!

For instance, the whole situation and its immediate antecedents took place in Jerusalem, where Paul was almost lynched because he was accused by the Jews of taking Trophimus the Ephesian into the temple. That was a false charge. He hadn't. Trophimus *was with* him, but Paul hadn't *taken* him into the temple. So you see Paul was thrown into prison on a bum rap, as we read in Acts 21:27-33. They were going to try to lynch him, but Paul's nephew got word of the plot, so the authorities sent him to Caesarea. There Paul was under what we today call protective custody, for two years. Actually, he was held because Felix, the governor, wanted money. Felix wanted his palm greased—something we are not unfamiliar with in our own time and generation.

We are also told that Festus, who succeeded Felix, hung

onto Paul because he wanted to please the Jews. So he kept him there on political grounds. Sounds familiar, doesn't it? For reasons of money, corruption, and political charges, Paul was kept in Caesarea. Then when they attempted to send him back to Jerusalem, he appealed to Caesar and was sent to Rome. On the way he was shipwrecked (a horrendous experience in itself), and now here he is in Rome for two years under house arrest, awaiting an uncertain verdict at the hands of a corrupt emperor.

In the face of all this, Paul says, "What has happened to me has happened for the progress of the gospel!" He saw the hand of God in his past, and he was able to bring that confidence to his present situation and circumstance. What an example for believers in all the following centuries!

What Might Have Been . . .

Are you stewing today, and I stewing today, about something in the past—about what might have been? "If only I had been here ten minutes sooner, or been there five minutes later. . . ." "If only I had said this or done that. . . ." "If only *she* had done this, that or the other thing. . . ." We drive ourselves wild with such second-guessing. Have you ever come to recognize, accept and be thankful for the providence of God in your past?

Do you know that the family into which you were born was of God and was not just something that happened by accident? Are you certain that the circumstances in which you find yourself now, whatever they may be, pleasant or difficult, are of God, and are not something that has happened by chance? That the personality you have—the abilities, the disabilities you have—are part of God's providential sovereignty? Or do you wish you were somebody else? Such a wish is not only futile, it's a misapprehension of a great truth.

Every one of us is who we are because God planned it that way. If you or I have failed, that's been part of God's overall providential sovereignty too. If you've been affected by other people's decisions, that too is part of God's providence. When others are involved in shaping our lives it may be particularly difficult to trust God and His providence. It's often easier to trust God about our own actions than it is to trust Him where other people take over decisions for us. But God's providence embraces those other people too. Even if we feel their decisions and motives are all wrong!

Not Kismet but Love

If you've learned to trust God in all your circumstances, it will take a lot of strain out of your life. If you never learn it you'll grind your teeth for the rest of your life and never find satisfaction. Now, when we talk about the providential sovereignty of God we're not talking about blind, inexorable fate that the Muslims call *kismet*. We're talking about a God who loves us with an everlasting love, a love that He demonstrated as dramatically as He possibly could through the Cross of Jesus Christ.

Our God is not a God who merely speaks propositionally about love. He is a God who has demonstrated His love in history, a God who numbers the hairs of our heads and who loves us. It's the love of a heavenly Father who has fashioned your past and mine. It's not blind fate; it's the providential sovereignty of the God who is alive and who cares.

Notice also that acceptance of the providential sovereignty of God does not imply passivity. We often have a false idea about God's sovereignty. "What will be, will be." "If it hits me, it hits me; if it doesn't hit me, it doesn't hit me." That concept we do not have in Scripture. That's fatalism.

Paul, as we see, was tremendously gripped by the true concept of the providential sovereignty of God, and he did not take life lying down. When Paul saw that he was going to be sent back to Jerusalem and would be involved with a hanging jury, so to speak, he appealed to Caesar. I personally do not think Paul missed the mind of God at all in this choice. He was exercising his right as a Roman citizen.

Singing at Midnight

When Paul and Silas were unjustly thrown into prison in Philippi (also part of God's providential sovereignty), they sang at midnight. Hearing them, the Philippian jailer got so shook he said, "What must I do to be saved?" And by morning he was converted. That day, when the authorities found out that Paul was a Roman citizen, they said, "Oh, very sorry, gentlemen; this was a police mistake, you know. If you don't mind, just sort of slip out of town and we'll forget the whole thing."

To that Paul replied, "Nothing doing, my dear friend. You threw us in here unjustly, so now you can come down to the magistrate and get us out of here publicly." Paul said this because he saw the implications of the event for the gospel to the rest of the Roman Empire. Besides that, he wanted it very clear that he had rights as a Roman citizen which could not be violated with impunity. Paul was not at all passive about what he knew was God's sovereign will.

We see another illustration of this attitude when Paul was shipwrecked. He took command—he didn't just allow the men to kill all the prisoners, as they were going to do. He took command and said, "Look, God has told me we're going to be saved. This is the way we're going to do it. Let's get to shore." Fortunately, they followed his advice.

Preventive Action

Life continually confronts us with situations about which we can do nothing. In those we must recognize the hand of God. But life also confronts us with situations about which we *can* take some action. In those we are not to be passive.

I've been in situations where Christians have presumed on the sovereignty of God. I was in a camp situation some years ago in which the whole thing was a shambles, and the leader kept saying, "Oh, well, we'll just trust the Lord and everything will be fine." I said, "What do you mean, trust the Lord? There are things we can do to bring ourselves out of this disastrous situation. God is not going to do for us what He expects us to do for ourselves. We've got responsibilities to take." And God did honor the *action* we took.

The sovereignty of God also involves our preventive action and our avoidance of evil. When it comes to temptation, we sometimes expect God to do something He has not promised to do. We must avoid walking into the jaws of a particular temptation and then saying, "Lord, do something!" If we do that we'll find ourselves asking God to deliver us from a temptation which we have the choice to walk away from ourselves.

The Jaws of Temptation

To walk right into the jaws of temptation and then say, "How come God didn't do something?" is like going halfway down a toboggan slide and then saying, "Lord, stop the toboggan!" He's never promised to do that.

We're repsonsible not to go to the top of the toboggan slide. Whatever area of temptation it is, we can't expect God on the basis of His power and providence to do something He has not promised to do. It may be some situation in our lives for which we should get professional help. *We* are to take initiative. Our trust in God's providential sovereignty means that when we see situations and circumstances that we can't do anything about, we acknowledge the hand of God in them. We accept them with thanksgiving without trying to fight them and without spending the rest of our lives second-guessing.

We also need to recognize that the sovereignty of God should not lead us to passivity in our current situation. Paul recognized that the hand of God in his past had brought him to that Roman prison. He was fruitful in the midst of his crisis. You or I might be in a crisis situation right now, but that doesn't mean we're on the shelf during that time, or that there is nothing God can do through us in the situation.

Why Me, Lord?

I see a number of reasons why Paul was spiritually productive even in this less-than-fortuitous circumstance. He wasn't calling attention to himself either out of pity or out of pride. In prison Paul did not languish thinking God had forgotten him. He didn't say, "Why me, Lord? You know what a great ministry I had in mind, so how come this has happened to me?" In fact he didn't see his situation as a problem at all. He realized he was there by divine appointment.

Those Roman guards probably thought they were put there to guard Paul, but in Philippians 1:16 Paul says, "I am put here for the defense of the gospel." Because Paul's prison situation was an appointment from God, there was no room for self-pity or second-guessing. He saw that the only really important fact was that he was where God wanted him to be.

Paul kept moving because he considered himself part of the "now" generation. Notice Philippians 1:20. He says, "It is my eager expectation and hope that I shall not be at all ashamed, but that with full courage, now as always, Christ will be honored in my body." He was living and witnessing for Christ *now*, not waiting for a better future.

Futuritis

A lot of us are plagued with "futuritis" in our Christian life and witness as well as in our desire to become men and women of God. We're going to begin "some other time," when it's more convenient. When we get this done and that settled, *then* we will start to do God's work. But somehow, we never get off the ground.

The only day you and I have to live is today. We've all heard that today is the first day of the rest of our lives. Have you vowed to be something for God? What steps will you take to become what you have vowed? Have you committed yourself to Him and begun to study the Word of God, really laying hold of God in prayer, praying for specific individuals by name?

If it's a matter of witnessing, the first step is to pick up the telephone and call somebody. Or walk around the corner and push a doorbell to begin building a bridge of friendship with a non-Christian neighbor. God wants us to take definite steps.

Paul operated in the present even though his situation was not the most auspicious that he could have imagined, or that he had already experienced up to that point. Paul saw the providence of God in his past, but he also saw it in his present situation.

The Praetorian Guard

Incredibly, Paul made the statement that his present situation was the means of the whole praetorian guard hearing the gospel. It was a phenomenal aspect of the providence of God that put Paul in this slot and gave him this opportunity. The praetorian guard was composed of crack troops who were rotated into the capital in Rome. Part of their duty was to guard prisoners who were going to be tried before Caesar, the emperor. At other times these troops were rotated throughout the whole of the Roman empire as elite soldiers with special privileges and special pay. Tradition tells us that some of these praetorian guards, who heard the gospel from Paul, eventually evangelized Britain when they were sent there.

You can just see Paul viewing this imprisonment as a

tremendous opportunity. As the first guard is chained to Paul, he starts talking with him, and before long he says, "By the way, are you interested in spiritual things?" And lo and behold he starts to talk to him about the Savior. (See How to Give Away Your Faith: Inter-Varsity Press). Before long the word undoubtedly begins to get around to the other guards, and the next few soldiers who come along start saying, "O.K., Paul, you can lay it on me now—we don't need a preamble." They're all set, expecting Paul to talk with them about Jesus Christ! Paul was never bashful in this kind of thing. So viable was Paul's witness that he could write, "It has become known throughout the whole praetorian guard and to all the rest that my imprisonment is for Christ."

Now let's remember that during this time in history we were not in the Jesus generation. *Time*, *Newsweek*, and NBC were not there, talking about the Jesus revolution and the street people. Christ was an unknown name. And for Paul to take this stand, to make this witness to Christ, and for it to have gained this circulation, is a phenomenal thing. It was not at all like our Christian-veneered society, with the media picking up Christianity and headlining it. In my judgment ours is perhaps the easiest time to witness in the twentieth century. And it is in sharp contrast to Paul's day. Yet he could write, "The whole praetorian guard has heard the gospel." And he could add, "Most of the brethren have been made more confident in the Lord."

Billy Graham or Paul?

Some Christians base their whole lives on a misconception. That is, "Boy, if Billy Graham isn't around we can't have any evangelism." Or "If the pastor of this or that church does this or that great thing, God is going to work." In the same vein, Christians of Paul's day had been thinking, "Wow! Paul's in Rome and we're going to have a great revival!" They were trusting in Paul. But he was taken right out from under them. And Paul said, "Great! The wonderful thing is, I've been clunked into prison."

The brethren were made confident, not in Paul, but *in the Lord*. And they suddenly realized that, lo and behold, God could and would speak through *them*! People were becoming converted as they did the communicating themselves. Some of these people evidently had mixed motives, yet God still honored the truthfulness of the message in spite of this.

Have you come to the place of confidence in the Lord, knowing that He can and will use *you* personally, and not just somebody on the staff of your church?

The great tragedy of the evangelical church in the twentieth century is that, as Howard Hendricks of Dallas Seminary says, it's like football—22 men on the field desperately in need of rest and 50,000 people in the stands desperately in need of exercise.

Do you believe that God could and would work through you in a neighborhood Bible study? "Oh, I should say not. I haven't been to seminary, I haven't done this, and I haven't done that." Where is your confidence? Is it in the Lord, or is it in your education or in some institution? Where is it? What do you really think God can and will do through you? Have you ever sat down and thought about that? "What could God do through me if I were to make myself available to Him?"

One of the Enemy's prime devices which I think is even more effective than getting us to think we're God's gift to humanity, is to wipe us out on the *other* side by overwhelming us with a sense of *inferiority*. "Oh, I can't do anything, I'm nothing, blah, blah, blah." It sounds tremendously spiritual, but it may be a denial of the grace of God who wants to work through you in Christ. You and I *are* something. By His grace He *can* and *will* work through us all, not just through those who are in the professional ministry. As Paul says, "*The brethren* wax confident in the Lord."

You and I can recognize the providential sovereignty of God in our lives right now. We can "wax confident" in the Lord and ask Him what He wants to do through us, either as part of the church program or in some other way. God has work for every one of us to do if we're willing to put ourselves at His disposal. God is willing to use every one of us; He's not limited to full-timers or to people with particular gifts. Every one of us has a spiritual gift of one kind or another. All we need to do is to crystallize it and put it into action.

Past, Present and Future

Paul saw the providential sovereignty of God not only in his past, but also in his immediate present—in what was happening right now. Therefore he was active even in the context of his adverse circumstances. And beyond that Paul also saw the providence of God in his *future*. That's what gave him rest and peace.

You know, some people drive themselves wild wishing what might have been in the past. Other people drive themselves frantic with worry about the future with all its uncertainties. Of course the future *is* uncertain, and boy, if you really let yourself think about it, it can really get to you. Left to ourselves, life is a kind of Russian roulette.

It's easy to see where the existentialist, apart from any frame of reference toward the loving sovereign God, would agree with Shakespeare's character who said, "Life is a tale told by an idiot, full of sound and fury, signifying nothing." From his point of view the only way to handle life is to come to recognize its absurdity and "live on the edge of the abyss." That's the prevailing philosophy of millions of people today—a philosophy of despair. But all of us who know Jesus Christ reject that philosophy. We know that our future is in God's hands, just as Paul knew it.

A Life or Death Decision

Paul was waiting for a life-or-death decision from Nero. He didn't know which it was going to be, though he apparently suspected that it would be life at this point. From all we know historically, Paul was released for a brief period of further ministry before he was finally rearrested and executed. But the important point is that Paul said, "I don't know the details of my life or my future, but that really doesn't bother me because I know that the ultimate end of my life is very definite and very secure in the hands of God." He said also, "Whether I'm going to live or die really isn't the crucial thing for me. To live is Christ, and to die is gain."

God in His providence might take my life or yours tomorrow morning. It could happen. On the other hand we may still be here thirty years from now. We're not going to go to be with Him one moment sooner than the time He chooses for that event. We know also that to be with Him is far, far better.

Like me, you may have read about the poor fellow on the West Coast who was hijacked twice in two days. He was on the hijacked plane that was flying from Oakland to Sacramento, and he was also on the hijacked plane that was to fly from San Francisco to San Diego the next day! He couldn't believe it. He said, "What are the chances that I would be a hostage two days in a row on two planes? It must be one in umpteen million!" But nevertheless he was the man. The odds come up for all of us. I've flown with people who really didn't know too much about the providential sovereignty of God. They are shaky!

I remember one passenger in particular. I really didn't mean to unnerve him, but here's what happened. We were flying from Dallas to Denver after several Electras had gone down, and the airlines were again tinkering with the engines. This fellow said, "What equipment is this?" And I replied, "I don't know, I think it's an Electra." The poor guy almost jumped out of the window without a parachute. We were over Amarillo at that time, and by the time we got over Pueblo they told us it was some other model, and he was greatly relieved.

To a truly trusting Christian such things are no big problem. We can know that our lives and our futures are in the hands of a God who is all-loving and all-powerful and all-wise. You can't get any greater combination than this in your life or in mine! We're in the hands of this kind of God, and this is what Paul knew. This is why he was able to rest contentedly in that prison with all its misery and discomfort and with all the uncertainty that went with his situation.

Paul, you could say, had been knocked down in the surf of life. You too may have been knocked down or you may be thrashing around today. I've been through some hard situations too, but the thing that has kept me, and which has given me the existential awareness that in the storms of life the anchor does hold, is this realization: in my past experiences, in my present situation, and in all the details of my future, God is in control.

No Accidents with God

Is there anything in your past that has caused you to be agitated today? If there has been, thank God for the fact that it has not happened by accident. As unpleasant as it may be from your standpoint, thank God for it and accept it from His hand. Has there been bitterness and resentment which have burned you up from the inside out? Have you recognized that God wants to work in your life right now, or are you still waiting for that next ideal situation instead of moving now in your present context, however confined it may be?

As for projections into the future with all its uncertainties, why not relax your mind about them too? These are not just hollow words, but the greatest reality that can be known in all of life. This reality comes through a personal encounter with Jesus Christ, the living Lord. He has lived in history, has died and risen again, and now lives within us by the Holy Spirit. He is in total control.

The surf of life, however turbulent it may be, can be lived through, and we can get our feet back on terra firma as we come to grasp the same profound principle that Paul and so many other personalities of Scripture have learned. God grant that each of us may know the satisfaction, the comfort, the peace, and the power that come with full experiential awareness of this truth. Its awareness comes only to those who give away their lives to the right Person.

3

STEADFASTNESS IN GIVING AWAY YOUR LIFE

One year our family climbed up a hill overlooking Lake Michigan to watch Fourth of July fireworks soar into the air. Our efforts were rewarded as we saw them one after the other tear into the pitch black night with brilliant streaks of light. Some went very high and then burst into full umbrellas of light. Others, like the Roman rocket, exploded on the ground and immediately sent a dazzling display upwards. It was instant excitement but it soon fizzled out. While we watched, it hit me that some Christians are like those Roman rockets. They start out living full blast for God, serving the Lord, but three years later they're nowhere to be found. They've fizzled out.

Not everyone remains faithful to the end when they give away their lives to the Lord. But in God's sight, steadfastness and dependability are indispensable. He seeks persons whose word is their bond, not the Roman rocket type.

Most of us would agree with the statement that steadfastness is vital. Matthew reminds us, "He who endures unto the end will be saved." We remember dreaded examples in the Bible such as King Saul, who began with tremendous promise but ended up fighting against the Lord and committing suicide. We can think of others in this risky pattern—King Hezekiah, Ananias and his wife Sapphira and Judas Iscariot. In Revelation, chapter three, a whole church disappointed God because they became lukewarm. Their first rush of love had cooled noticeably, and God was sickened by it.

You may have acquaintances like this. I do. But the crux of the matter is that our primary responsibility is for our own steadfastness. And that can be pretty scary. We can find clues to help us in the biblical examples of people who remained faithful, but it's obvious that we answer individually to God alone. On top of that, we will not be excused for not enduring to the end on the basis of old age or long service already rendered. God intends us to be steadfast as long as we live on the earth!

Well, the point of this discussion is *not* discouragement but finding some helps. First of all, there are some clear *reasons* why steadfastness wanes. Second, there are some very reliable and God-directed *solutions* to the problem. And finally, our Lord has provided *incentives* to keep us steadfast and to help improve our batting average.

Weariness

In considering the reasons why steadfastness wanes, common ordinary physical weariness should be the first to check out. When we've been "on the road" in the Lord's service for a long time it is easy to feel, "I've done my job. I've worked hard for many years. I'd like to give up the ghost!" Does this sound familiar to you?

From weariness comes a loss of joy in the Lord's service. We take on a responsibility brimming with enthusiasm and expectation. Then, *thud.* It turns out to be a drag. We begin to say, "Ugh, how can I go through this again? I wish someone else would do it." Or in really desperate times we dream about moving away to start all over again and get out from under all the pressure. I've had these feelings at times myself. It's a common condition. All the while, there is the consciousness that God intends us to be joyful. And joy can't be faked. The life and service for Christ which should be completely exhilarating and exciting ends up an unbearable burden.

The Word of God says clearly that we should not be weary in well doing, for in due season we shall reap if we faint not. If we haven't been reaping, let's ask ourselves if we're just plain weary in doing. We may not have done anything wrong but have simply collapsed by the wayside from sheer fatigue.

Legalism

Next, let's ask ourselves whether we've ever jockeyed with God. Or ever tried to set up a bargain with Him? "I'll do this for You, Lord, and I know You'll have something good for me."

Maybe you're saying, "Who, me? What do you mean? I'm a Christian, saved by grace!" Well, of course, none of us would bargain with God consciously, but after a certain amount of weariness, a kind of incipient legalism takes over. We feel the progressive grip of obligations and strictures upon us to perform well. The very suggestion horrifies a Bible-taught Christian. "Salvation by grace through faith" is our byword. Yes, that's true, and few of us have problems with legalism or bargaining when it comes to salvation. We know that anybody who is going to have eternal life will get it as a free gift from God. But when it comes to rewards for Christian service, well. . . .

Too often we fail to see that living and maintaining the Christian life is *also* by grace through faith. Living for Christ is a free gift in the same sense that salvation is. It's unfortunate that without realizing it, we slip over into a legalistic framework. Each morning we read the Bible because we're afraid that assured disaster will come if we don't. We undertake Christian service because we think this is the only way to receive the blessing of the Lord. Prayer turns into a meaningless form. Going to church becomes a duty we've got to perform. And if everything isn't rosy and smooth we conclude the Lord has let us down.

This is the *quid pro quo*, this for that mentality, with reference to all kinds of Christian service. It's legalism. And its acids lap at our souls so that Christian activities become a drag. It's easy to see that this plays havoc with our steadfastness.

Other Christians Sour Us

Another thing that gets us off the track is the actions of other people. The ones who do public preaching or do the leading all look so enviable. "Wouldn't it be great to be like them? They must be on the top of the spiritual totem pole." Well, we may think this but that's not really true. The work and talents of the person on the platform is of no more value to God than the worship of the person in the pew who is living for Christ in his own place.

The whole matter concerning what other people are doing leads us to honestly admit that some of the Christians we know haven't been the most sensational examples of Christian virtue in the world. One or two of these may even have personally let us down or slandered us. We may begin to suspect they are phonies, hypocrites. If most of our friends and associates are confined to Christian circles, it tends to magnify the sour impressions, because we see most clearly the imperfections of the people closest to us.

Then, all of a sudden, people outside the Christian framework appear to have greater sparkle. "Those people outside the church are really having a ball. I think they are actually more genuine, down to earth people than the ones I've known in the church." But now our focus is turned on people, and not on the peerless Man, Jesus Christ. The result is that the wonder of knowing the Savior and the firm perseverance in His service languishes.

From this point, the complaining begins. "I've been

teaching this Sunday School class for five years and the kids still fidget. I've been setting up chairs for the meetings for twelve years and nobody seems to appreciate a thing I've done. I've taken care of the library and then gone to prayer meeting every week for ten years. Other people haven't. What do I have to show for it? I wonder if the whole thing is worthwhile."

Slow Leaks in the Christian Life

During a lecture at the University of Illinois, a Christian student in his senior year asked to talk to me. He told me his story of a progressive downward course in his Christian life, starting when he was a freshman, until now, in his final year, he was making no attempt to think about the Lord at all. He said it wasn't anything special that hit him but a kind of creeping coolness, like being caught in a gradual slide. One or two isolated sins settled in as strong habits. As a result, he lost any semblance of steadfastness. While he talked, I could see that collapse in the Christian life is never a blow-out; it's always a slow leak.

What could have started the process for that fellow? We talked about "the lusts of the flesh" as one category the Bible warns against. I suggested that he check his heart against the list in Galatians 5:19-21. Was this how he had lost his steadfastness? Self-indulgence, immorality, drunkenness, or some kind of impurity? Or greed? Greed is not always recognized, but it may stand at the top of the list of prevalent sins in contemporary America—never having enough. As a society we seek more and more pleasure, more and more gadgets, finer and larger homes.

Another category of sins that came up in the discussion was the sins of the spirit. One of these is bitterness that eats at our vitals. Someone may have said or done something to us that keeps rankling for days or months or years. Even if we were spiritually right in the situation and the other person totally wrong, if we continue to harbor resentment and hurt we will be wiped out eventually. This is the meaning of Hebrews 12:15: "See to it that . . . no 'root of bitterness' spring up and cause trouble and by it the many become defiled."

The young man said he saw some of these were true for him and he wanted to get back to where he had a constant walk of love and fellowship with his Lord. What a refreshing thing to hear. I knew the Lord heard the cry of his heart when he prayed.

Bitterness can come when tragedy strikes. Life may bring illness, accidents, handicaps, financial reverses, disappointments, or attacks on our reputations, but come what may it need not bring us bitterness too. In fact, bitterness is sin even if it is occasioned by some legitimate cause or unfair treatment. But we cannot overestimate its corrosive effect. I knew a man years ago who was in active service for the Lord. He allowed bitterness to completely change the course of his life. Even as an old man, he still nursed the grudge and was shriveled and wasted inside.

The Bible relentlessly exposes other internal sins too: pride, jealousy, covetousness, discontent, self-pity, self-centeredness, self-consciousness. These are soul-shrinking sins. And any person in their grip is described as being tossed helplessly by waves in a raging sea. When we give in to such sins, our trust in God is eroded, and before we know it, we want to give up and drop out.

So far, I have generally listed four reasons for loss of steadfastness. These seem to follow a certain sequence. Instead of responding to Christ out of love, we get weary and lose our joy. Then we take on a pattern of legalism in living the Christian life, we become offended by the actions and criticisms of other Christians, and finally we allow sin to pull us away from fellowship with Christ Himself. The end finds us questioning the worth and value of it all.

This is a pretty bleak picture. Did you ever get the impression that preachers do nothing but rail and tear down the listeners? The Bible itself furnishes some "Thou shalt nots." However, the negatives are just a very small part of God's message to us. Laced between the negatives are glorious promises and solid helps for us to use. And as you would expect, when God helps, He gets to the root of the matter.

The Cures

Now, let's take a look at the cures. Take weariness. If you need rest, block out some time and take it! Physical fatigue can completely distort our perspective. A. W. Tozer prescribed twenty-four hours of undisturbed sleep as the first step to cure discouragement. It's surprising how many problems lighten after a good period of rest. Try it! Then, don't be afraid to change what you are doing. It might give you a new perspective. Often when you make a fresh start, other people will get inspired to pitch in and help. New avenues could open up for you as well. Take definite steps.

First: Open Yourself to God's Love

If legalism sets in, contemplate God's love for you as an individual. When I turn my mind to His love for me, I'm staggered. He loved me and gave His life for me even before I knew anything about Him. He loves me now. And He will continue to love me. It couldn't be expressed any better than in John 15:13: "Greater love has no man than this, that a man lay down his life for his friends."

The magnitude of the death of Christ can be appreciated only when we recognize with deep conviction that we are sinners. Besides that, we have the potential for even the grossest of sins. We know intellectually that Romans 3:23 tells us we all have sinned. Yet we who have grown up in the church, have never been out "in the far country" of rebellion and worldliness may affirm that fact only propositionally and not experientially. We agree with the statement about our condition but find it hard to recognize the potential for sin and corruption within our own hearts. Consequently, it is not so easy to appreciate the reason why Christ had to die on the cross. I've had this kind of Christian background myself and I know that I must not allow the significance of His death for me to become commonplace.

Isaiah had the kind of experience we need. When he saw the Lord "high and lifted up," he said, "Woe is me, for I am a man of unclean lips" (Isaiah 6:1, 5). See the sequence? He saw the holiness of the Lord. Then he saw the corruption of his own heart. Peter knew this too. The Lord arranged a miraculous catch of fish for the disciples. Peter was overwhelmed with astonishment. He knelt at Jesus' feet. He could have said, "Thank you." He could have said, "You're wonderful, Lord." He could have said a number of things. He didn't. He said, "Depart from me, Lord, for I am a sinful man."

Perhaps the only reason some of us haven't succumbed to some sins is that we have never been faced with that temptation. Truly seeing the Lord Jesus, God's Son, means realizing our own corruption. Then and only then can we see the love He expressed for us on the cross. To overcome legalism we need to recognize the love of God for us in the death of Christ. Here we can comprehend, however minutely, what a privilege it is to be His servant.

Second: What Do You Want to Accomplish in Life?

Stop here and think what you would like your life to add up to at its final end. You'd probably want it to have had some deep significance, to have had it really count for something. Not just years of playing games. You'd also probably like to think your life had made an impact on people around you and made some changes in the world. You'd even like to think that those changes would last beyond the time your body went into its grave.

Steadfastness in Giving Away Your Life

I recently heard Studs Turkel on television talking about his book, *Working*. In that book Turkel compiled a collection of almost every conceivable kind of work opportunity. For each job he told the advantages, polled from people who have done the job. His conclusion after all the research was that the single, most sought-after component in a job is *meaning*. Endlessly putting bolts in a handle or fenders on a car or stamps on receipts or any other repetitious monotony is done only to be forgotten. Shuffling papers in an office or a bank will not be remembered or recognized the way a fireman's saving a child's life is remembered. Turkel's conclusion has never left me: each person is absorbed in a search for meaning.

Many people work daily in jobs that don't really amount to much. And they know it. It's downright discouraging to be caught in an endless rut of drudgery. But believers in Jesus Christ need never to be in a rut. If I were trying to dream up a satisfying life, I couldn't conceive of any greater plan than the privilege of doing what every Christian has the opportunity to do—communicate the message of life, the good news of Jesus Christ.

Just project what this means to people whose lives are purposeless, hopeless, aimless, without knowing God personally. The youngest and newest Christian can share Jesus Christ. He alone can meet man's deepest longings and aspirations. He can change entrenched and stubborn habit patterns. He can even break every chain of sin. This is what brings the longed-for purpose and significance. It's a life that neither money nor prestige can buy.

There is nothing I would rather do in all the world than communicate God's good news, to see individuals touched by the Holy Spirit and brought into fellowship with the Savior. It's astounding to watch new Christians change as their knowledge of Jesus Christ grows. And the added bonus is knowing that we are all going to be in heaven forever. I can't think of any other occupation that offers such compensation, such fringe benefits!

Soak in the love of Christ every day and be refreshed by Him. Give praise to Him daily for each event that He brings into your life. That's the way out of legalism and the bad of habit of jockeying with God. Just say, "Thank You, Lord, for the privilege of serving You today in whatever way You choose."

Third: What Does God Want You to Do?

It's easy to become preoccupied with what others do or what they think. What "they" do and what "they" think cuts into us in such depth. The great achievers make us envious, and the failures make us critical. How do we stop worrying about what other Christians are doing?

The answer lies in getting back to God's basic goal for each of us as individuals. That goal is to do *all* for God's glory. Sounds good and theological, but how do I arrive at that place from where I am?

To start with, ask God Himself, "What do *You* want me to do, Lord?" After all, we are playing on His team. He is the leader and He has a unique work for each of us to do with our talents and background. The winner of the Super Bowl is a team. Each member has a different function. If they all tried to be quarterbacks they'd be in real trouble. They need tackles, tailbacks, running backs, *et al.* Each is indispensable and each has his own plays. In God's Super Bowl we are all equally indispensable. And God, the Leader, calls the plays.

I find help in looking at the variety of people that God used in the Bible. Lydia manufactured and sold purple dye. Amos herded sheep. The Apostle Paul made tents. Luke was a doctor. Several of the disciples were fishermen. Some of these continued their occupations while they served the Lord.

If you are a mother in a home, you serve the Lord by keeping your home going smoothly. If that is God's will for you it means as much in His sight as teaching a class or writing a book. The same is true if you work in a shop, or if you are a teacher or a student. If you are where God wants you to be, doing your service for Christ and witnessing for Him there, you are in no way inferior to the person in full-time service. Let God show you where He wants you—that will eliminate the second guesses—and go on from there.

Fourth: Do All for God's Glory

Ephesians chapter six says that we are able to work at our jobs and serve Christ, too. "Slaves, be obedient to those who are your earthly masters, with fear and trembling, in singleness of heart, as to Christ; not in the way of eyeservice, as men-pleasers, but as servants of Christ, doing the will of God from the heart, rendering service with a good will as to the Lord and not to men, knowing that whatever good anyone does, he will receive the same again from the Lord, whether he is a slave or free" (verses 5-8). What a challenge! Whatever I am doing, I can do it for the glory of God. This transforms the most routine things in life.

To pinpoint this, Paul says, "Whether you eat or drink, do all to the glory of God." Did you ever think that eating and drinking can be to God's glory? These aren't actually spiritual activities, but our attitude in doing them can make them spiritual. As each detail of life is lived to the glory of God, then the whole of life takes on eternal significance.

Fifth: Results Will Come

The book of Timothy gives another clue to help us. He says that it's the hardworking farmer who ought to have the first share of the crops. Let's think about the farmer. He goes out and sows the seed. But he doesn't see results overnight. He doesn't go out the next morning and say, "I wonder if all that sowing and fertilizing was worthwhile." A week later he doesn't go back again and moan, "Nothing's up yet." If he didn't know about seeds and growing crops, he might give up. But he knows that it takes time. Something is happening in the ground even though it cannot be seen. In the same way, a Christian may not immediately see tangible spiritual results in what he is doing, but God assures him that without a shadow of a doubt, in the future, fruit will come!

Sixth: Why It Is Possible to Continue

The question of the worthwhileness of serving God came to me with new force the day I got the news that my Dad had gone to be with the Lord. He was hospitalized in Chicago while I was in Los Angeles for a meeting at the Airport Marina Hotel. The night before, when I had talked to him on the phone, he was cheerful and encouraged. The doctors had told him he was recovering exceptionally well from his heart attack and could go home in a few days. I suggested that he come to our home for a time of recovery. His reply was, "Oh, no. I can go right home. And I can drive myself home from the hospital." After a heart attack!

As you can imagine, it was a shock to get a phone call from my wife the next day that he'd had another attack. At that time, the attack did not appear fatal. But a half hour later, another call brought the crushing message that even if I flew back immediately, I would not see him alive.

For the next hour I sat in my hotel room. I thought, I prayed, I cried. Where can one go at such a time? The Lord brought some Scriptures to my mind. In the twenty-first chapter of Revelation, I read the promise that in God's prepared place there will be no more sickness, no crying, no tears. I also read and reread the familiar words about death from 1 Corinthians 15: "For this perishable nature must put on the imperishable, and this mortal nature must put on immortality. When the perishable puts on the imperishable, and the mortal must put on immortality, then shall come to pass the saying that is written: 'Death is swallowed up in victory.' 'O Death, where is thy victory? O Death, where is thy sting?' The sting of death is sin, and the power of sin is the law. But thanks be to God, who gives us the victory through our Lord Jesus Christ" (verses 53-57).

I was familiar with this passage and had often quoted the following verse, in which the Apostle Paul says, "My beloved brethren, be steadfast, immovable, always abounding in the work of the Lord, knowing that in the Lord your labor is not in vain" (verse 58). But until that morning I had never seen the connection between the two thoughts: first, that mortal man shall certainly put on immortality, causing death to lose its sting; and second, because of this promise we need never lose heart. We know we have a future beyond the grave. We can continue to be steadfast.

This was the Lord's word of comfort to me: "All is O.K. Dad is in heaven and though you are still here, you will one day experience what he is already experiencing. In the meantime, be steadfast, immovable. Abound in the work of the Lord."

We are all investing in eternity, building up our inheritance each day that we serve the Lord Jesus Christ. And that is the greatest investment available in all the earth. The promise comes from God Himself.

Seventh: Check All Leaks

The final solution to consider is to plug the gradual leaks that let sin into our lives. First, we must ask Him to show us the holes in our defenses—those places where temptation is likely to enter. Then we need to confess these gaps and ask Him for strength to seal them up. An absolute loathing of all sin is God's work within us, delivering us. In this way we resist the Devil so that he will flee from us.

The battle against sin of all kinds is won in the mind. Charles Spurgeon said, "As I look within my heart, I realize that I am capable of anything apart from the grace of God which keeps me day by day." Everything we do or say begins with a thought. A sin that is not conquered in the mind will manifest itself in an act. That's why Proverbs gives the advice, "Keep your heart with all diligence; for from it flow the springs of life" (4:23).

The antidote to the leaks of sin is to take the attitude David expressed in Psalm 16:8, and to exercise it everyday. He declared, "I keep the Lord always before me; because He is at my right hand, I shall not be moved." David wrote these tremendous words when he was being hunted like a criminal by King Saul and his troops. He knew that God had anointed him to be the next king, so he refused to be dismayed by his circumstances. His mind and heart were set on the Lord. But what did he mean by setting the Lord before him? Undoubtedly, he thought about the Lord before everything else; he meditated on the Lord and His sovereignty. David saw all of the circumstances of life through that glass, so to speak. When the crunch came he was not moved from his position of faith. With God in the forefront of his thinking, he had inner stability.

Incentives

We have examined some of the solutions to the problem of loss of steadfastness. Now the Lord provides realistic incentives to motivate us.

The first incentive to be steadfast is His promise to use every one of us if we will let Him. Every Christian has this potential. Do you honestly believe this? The promise that God will use us, as expressed in 2 Corinthians 4:7, is that every one of his children has "this treasure in earthen vessels, to show that the transcendent power belongs to God and not to us." The treasure is ministry and service for our Lord, showing others the glory of God and the glorious

Gospel of Christ. We may feel common and useless, but we need no greater qualification than that of a clay jar; then He can use us.

Our purpose is to show forth His splendid power, not our own talents. In fact, another section of 1 Corinthians says that God chooses those who are weak, foolish and of little strength. But we contain His excellent and glorious power. Do we really need anything else? Make yourself available to Him!

Spiritual Gifts

The second incentive is the assurance that every one of us has one or more spiritual gifts to be developed for this work. Again, the book of 1 Corinthians tells us about these. There are varieties of gifts with the same Spirit and there are varieties of service, but the same Lord. And there are varieties of working but it's the same God who inspires them all in every one of us. God bestows gifts on every Christian.

When we speak of a gifted believer we tend to think of somebody who can lead a class or organize a program. That *is* a gift which not everyone has. However, it's only one of the gifts. There are many others. Have you ever prayed, "Lord, what is the gift you have given me?" Let us not go through years of life without pinpointing the specific gifts God has given us. It's possible to go through life and never recognize our gifts, never be thankful, and never stir them up. Let's do a little stirring. Let's use our gifts so they can develop and accomplish what God wants them to accomplish.

Whatever our gifts are, they are for the "common good," to benefit the whole church (1 Corinthians 12:7). For example, the Peninsula Bible Church of Palo Alto, California is making a great impact in that city. One reason for its outstanding ministry is that its pastor, Ray Stedman, has taught the people that each of them has one or more gifts for the work of the church, and that the pastor is not to do all the work. Everybody is involved. He helped them discover their gifts, and then they use them. Some have the gift of evangelism, some of help, some of administration. So the church really goes places! They conduct at least a hundred Bible studies in the area, many of which are at Stanford University. The members have appropriated the truth of the Scripture teaching and have developed gifts for the common good.

The way to discover our gifts is to jump in and try things. If you try to lead a Bible study and nobody knows what you're talking about, that could be a good indication that teaching is not your gift. But try again. Don't give up after one attempt. Remember, a gift must be developed. If, after a few more tries, it still sounds like Greek to your hearers (and you're not speaking in Greek), then your gift lies somewhere else.

Pray for direction. You may have the gift of wisdom, of disciplining, of counseling, of exercising faith, or of showing mercy. And there are others. I believe many more of us have the gift of evangelism than we think. The reason we have never discovered it, is that we have not gone out and evangelized. When we begin to make friends we see God the Holy Spirit opening our mouths. As we talk about our faith openly and honestly, we find that God brings results.

To develop a gift takes time. The first time I was asked to speak at a weekend conference, the thought of four hour-long lectures almost paralyzed me. I spent hours laboring over those talks, terrified that I would run out of material. As time went on, I had so much to share that I became more concerned about running out of *time* than running out of material. First efforts may be weak and stumbling, but gifts grow as the Holy Spirit is able to possess more of our beings. The verse we started with was that the splendid power belongs to God and not to us. We are but the common container for that power.

Another point to consider regarding gifts is the linear concept of Christian service. If we begin a particular work at one stage in our lives, we are not automatically boxed into that form of service for the rest of our lives. Obviously there are many kinds of things we can do when we're single and twenty-one that we can't do when we're married and thirty-one. It's just a simple fact of life. When we accept the responsibility of a family, we automatically accept some limitations along with the expanding scope of life that comes with being parents.

After our children have grown up and left home, new opportunities appear. With increasing age our capacities and talents change. A sixty-year-old man may not have the strength for a job he started at age twenty. On the other hand, he will have developed skills through the experiences of life that will equip him for things he could not have done at twenty or thirty or forty.

Regardless of our age, it is God's will that we "endure" and continue to minister to others. In Chicago I became acquainted with an old man named Harry Major. One day I introduced Mr. Major to my children. "This is Harry Major," I said. "He's ninety-two." The man was insulted! "No, no," he protested. "I'm ninety-*five*!"

Just watching that man encouraged me. Talk about steadfastness! When he showed up at a meeting, God blessed the rest of us by his very presence and enthusiasm. Every day he rode the elevated train to Chicago's "loop" to counsel people on the telephone at Victory Servicemen's Center.

It's possible that we are not able to do as much active work as someone else, but we still can pray. We still can love. Just being faithful, like Harry Major, generates enthusiasm in people who can work in ways that we cannot.

Praying Is Everyone's Gift

Prayer for others is a privilege at any age. Sometimes we

think, "I used to be very active, but I don't have the physical strength anymore." But what about prayer? You might select one or two young people in your church and pray for each of them by name every day. If you get to know each other well, a relationship of love and care develops. Of course, you should not expect perfection from them. But you can accept them, love them, and enter into their spiritual battles. And then you'll enter also into their victories.

Mature Christians don't pray, "Lord, bless the whole world." Vague, general prayers are not effective. But we can "adopt" one missionary family as our friends, get to know them, and learn what their special needs are. Then we can pray for them specifically, and as we write letters to them and enter into their work, we can share in their lives, whether their concern at a given time is some aspect of their work or some aspect of their private family lives. We can carry their load with them!

Finally, praise God, our service is not limited to our own resources. If the whole thing depended on us, it would be hopeless. But God never intends for us to undertake anything for Him in our own strength. Paul says, "I don't count myself as sufficient for anything . . . our sufficiency is of God, who has qualified us to be ministers of the new covenant" (2 Corinthians 3:5-6). And in Philippians 4:13 he says, "I can do all things through Him who strengthens me."

These promises are not shibboleths or clichés. They are experiential realities of great power. When we take action to involve ourselves in serving Jesus Christ steadfastly, His power is released through us on a supernatural plane. This Christian life is not a natural, ordinary life; it's God's holy action through us! That's what makes it powerful. That's what makes it rhapsodic. It's not just a question of pulling ourselves together and doing the best we can. It's opening our whole beings to God so that He lives His life through us.

However, service and activity are not the same thing. Periodically we need to ask ourselves, "Am I in the thick of activity because *God* has put me here, or have I just slipped into an endless merry-go-round, accomplishing nothing?"

If you're in a rat race, get out of it long enough to say, "Lord, what service do *You* want me to undertake? What area of witness or of prayer? To whom can I show love and hospitality for Your sake? Where can I get involved in sharing Your Word with someone? Where do you want me to invest my money in Your service? Lord, give me a steadfast, Spirit-led attitude in giving away my life to You."

4

SPIRITUAL REALITY IN GIVING AWAY YOUR LIFE!

Some time ago on the West Coast a friend of mine took a non-Christian with him to a Christian young people's group. As they left the meeting, my friend said to his companion, "Well, what did you think?" The man's reply was very interesting, "In that group there were some people who have it, and some people who don't."

What was the "it" they were talking about? The two friends had been discussing what it is to become a Christian and have true Christian reality. They had seen this quality of reality in only some of the members of the group. It's eye-opening to observe how instinctively non-Christians can tell whether we've got the goods or not. They can see through a spiritual phony like a pane of glass. We can say all the right spiritual words, but they will intuitively pick up whether Jesus Christ is truly the driving force and passion of our lives.

Some people may make this same observation when they come into our churches and fellowships—there are some people who have it and there are others who don't. Genuine reality is strikingly obvious even though the external actions may be homogeneous.

Reality not Fantasy

It's this spiritual reality that I'd like you to think about with me in giving away your life. Though it is critically important that we Christians be *relevant* in our daily living (if we aren't, people will simply ignore us), it is equally important that there be the ring of spiritual reality in our lives. This is what brings us true joy, genuine fellowship with other Christians and a positive impact on those around us who need our Savior. Malcolm Muggeridge said it cryptically from his own experience, "The world is full of fantasy; there must be reality somewhere and the only reality that I've found is the reality of the Christian faith."

Two statements about two men in the Old Testament give us important clues as to what spiritual reality is and what it is not. In this chapter we'll consider the first one found in Judges 16:20. It has to do with Samson. Samson, as you may recall, was a man who had great privileges. He knew God and His power. But somewhere along the line he had lost his spiritual reality because he took many of his blessings for granted. Eventually he even came to the place of toying with God and His truth.

You probably remember how Samson in disobedience to God married Delilah, and then how Delilah taunted him trying to find the secret of his strength. Well, Samson finally divulged to her the information and she promptly communicated it to his Philistine enemies. This was all they needed to capture him, but God intervened at the last moment and spared his life. Yet, Samson still didn't get the message and came to the final disaster recorded in Judges 16:20: "And she said, 'The Philistines are upon you, Samson!' And he awoke from his sleep and said, 'I will go out as at other times, and shake myself free.' And he knew not that the Lord had left him."

That's a chilling phrase to me: he didn't realize that the Lord had departed from him! Samson said the same words and did the same things he had always done. But now there was something different about him, and that something was that the Lord had departed from him. It was easy to see it in the sad results.

The same thing may be true of us. Externally there may not be much observable difference, but eventually it becomes evident that the Lord is no longer with us in the way He once was.

The Privilege and the Danger

The irony in the Christian life is that sometimes those things that are the greatest advantage to us, we may view as an impediment. For example, the privilege of being raised in a Christian home. This was my background. (Some of you know that my father, Robert J. Little, was the late radio pastor of station WMBI in Chicago.) Of all the families I could have been born in, I'm thankful I chose to be born in this one!

Though it is a great privilege to be raised in a Christian home, there are also a number of subtle dangers to guard against. For instance, from the earliest times we can remember, many of us have believed things about the Lord Jesus Christ just because our parents told them to us, and we had confidence in our parents. We heard these things in church and Sunday school, and we gave mental assent to the facts. Yet somewhere along the line, with some of us, there has never been that decision of personal, thoughtful commitment to Christ. Almost unconsciously, we think we can ooze into the Kingdom of God because we have never known a time when we didn't believe.

Don't misunderstand me—I'm not saying that we have to be able to name the day and the hour and the moment we crossed that line. Without knowing the exact day, we can know indisputably that we belong to Christ today because he is the driving force of our lives. But when we're raised in a Chrisitan home, it is dangerously possible to blend in with the woodwork, assume that we're Christians, and even persuade other people that we are, without ever really *being* Christians!

Sweeter than the Day Before?

Along with this, from the earliest times we can remember, we have sung hymns and choruses that are far beyond the reality of our spiritual experience. We sing about every day with Jesus being sweeter than the day before, but the question is, "Is this an experience that's real to me?" As little children we sing, "I'm so happy, and here's the reason why: Jesus took my burdens all away." Now these words are wonderful if they're true in our experience, but they could be far beyond true reality.

We also sing hymns of commitment that go beyond the depth of our actual intention: "Take my life and let it be consecrated, Lord, to Thee." We sing that with great enthusiasm, but it may represent something that has never actually taken place in our lives. If so, we find ourselves with a consciously increasing gap between what we say with our lips and what we live out in our lives.

One of the most solemn statements in the Word of God is found in Matthew 7:21: "Not everyone who says to me, 'Lord, Lord,' shall enter the kingdom of heaven, but he who does the will of my Father who is in heaven." This is talking about people who say all the right words, sing all the right hymns, go to all the right places, and avoid doing all the wrong things, yet are never born into the family of God.

The people Jesus referred to in that verse just blended into the woodwork. We may too. So we do well to think about our own experience of salvation. A personal, deliberate commitment of ourselves to the Lord Jesus Christ as a living Person is the beginning.

No Grandchildren

It has been said that God has no grandchildren. Very

true. Parents can assume their children are born again. Children likewise may assume they have inherited their parent's faith. But neither can act for the other. Each individual must come because of his own will and desire for the Lord's grace.

Obedience—a deep desire to obey Him—is the key indication that we have come into new and genuine life in Christ. The explanation of why merely calling "Lord, Lord," is not enough is given in the following phrase: we must do the will of the Father who is in heaven. Genuine calling on the Lord results in "doing." In the same vein, John says, "By this we may be sure that we know Him, if we keep His commandments," I John 2:3. We keep His commandments not as the means by which we achieve salvation, but as the sure evidence that we have had the transforming experience of the new birth. Obedience is the evidence that we are new creatures in Christ, that the old attitudes have been changed, and that new things have come to us through Christ.

No Faith to Lose

In an incisive magazine article entitled "No Faith to Lose," Dr. John Scanzoni probes the problem of young people who go off to secular college campuses and apparently lose their faith. The real problem, he points out, is that they never had any viable faith to lose in the first place!

Dr. Scanzoni suggests that there are actually three levels of faith—indoctrination faith, conformity faith, and commitment faith. And he shows that only the last of these is genuine, New Testament faith that results in the new birth.

The person with *indoctrination faith* absorbs all the information about Christ, but he does not in honesty commit himself to the Lord. Such faith can fade in the face of a hostile challenge.

The person with *conformity faith* acts as a Christian because of social pressure pushed on him from the outside.

But he does not have a spontaneous desire within. This kind of faith is likely to be lost once the external pressure to conform is removed.

Commitment Faith

But the real thing is *commitment faith.* Life in the Lord Jesus—being a real Christian—is not merely giving mental assent to propositional facts about the Lord Jesus Christ. It is *repentance of sin and commitment to a living Person.* The rub comes because sin shows up largely in a desire to live independently from God. But Christianity is not a "Philosophy 72" college course as opposed to "Agnosticism 13" or "Existentialism 22," any more than marriage is "Philosophy 77" as opposed to "Singlehood 12"! Marriage is not a philosophy. You can believe all about marriage, you can read books on marriage, you can go to the weddings of a dozen of your friends, but that's still not going to make you married.

One thing is absolutely crucial for marriage, and that is *personal commitment to a person.* You must receive a person into your life and enter into a consulting relationship about everything else from then on. And that is exactly what is involved in the kind of faith that saves. We enter into a dependent relationship with Christ, in which every area of our lives comes under His consulting care.

Rightly understood, a Christian home can lead to a wonderful, deep-rooted understanding of God's word. It can introduce the young person to Christian work early in his life. It can prepare the ground for life-long habits of walking with the Lord and purity of life. It can be a priceless privilege.

The Christian School

Another environment that could lead us to the same situation as Samson is the Christian school. As you may know, I spend much of my time on secular university campuses, and I meet an alarming number of young people who have been through very fine Christian schools but still have not had a genuine Christian experience. I believe that none of us is immune from the temptation of settling for a superficial conformity of any type.

The tremendous advantage of a Christian environment carries with it some inherent pitfalls by its very nature. When the Word of God is taught day by day and we are in continuous fellowship and contact with Christian people, we can easily become victims of environmental Christianity. By this I mean the subtle tendency to depend on the people and the activities in which we live for personal sustenance, rather than on firsthand, direct contact with the living God Himself.

If we succumb to this easy temptation, our faith can falter when this environment is stripped away (as it must inevitably be). It's a privilege to be in the Christian school setting, to have the Word of God opened to us in chapel and to hear it over the radio, but if everything is secondhand for us rather than firsthand, our Christian experience will be only stale and unreal.

Your First-Hand Data

I'll never forget what Charles Troutman told about a conversation with an agnostic in the student union at McGill University in Montreal. The student came over and said to Charles very bluntly and plainly, "What does Jesus Christ mean to you personally?"

As Charles relates it, "I replied with a wonderful story I had once heard in chapel of how God had delivered a missionary in the upper headquarters of the Amazon." The agnostic responded, "I beg your pardon. I said, what does Jesus Christ mean to *you*?" Charles continued, "I told him another story about somebody I had heard of in Africa and what God had wonderfully done in his life." And the non-

Christian repeated again, "I beg your pardon, I didn't ask what He meant to *other* people, I asked you what He means to *you*." Charles recalls, "Suddenly I realized that I had robbed myself of my own firsthand data of the Christian life, without which what I had to say meant very little."

Do you have firsthand data in your Christian life today, or are you in the danger zone in which Samson found himself—of not being aware that the Lord had departed from him? I have known this, and the struggle that accompanies it. The irony is that in some ways it's harder to prove the reality of the Lord in a warmly Christian atmosphere than it is when we're out in the front lines of the battle!

Hanging on the Straps

For several years I lived in New York City. I can remember hanging onto the subway straps on the way to New York University. I'd be praying, "O Lord, You know those students I'm to meet with, and You know their attitude and how difficult it is for me. Lord, You help me, because I'm a goner unless You undertake for me." Believe me, I was desperate!

Then I had the privilege of doing some graduate study in a Christian school. What a contrast! I got up with Christians, I brushed my teeth with Christians, I studied with Christians, I went to chapel with Christians, I ate lunch with Christians, I played ping-pong with Christians.

It was sensational until about the middle of November, when it suddenly dawned on me that the Lord was not as real to me as He was when I was hanging onto those straps in New York City. I had to get before God and say, "Lord I believe You can be as real and as vital and as personal to me here in this uncommonly pleasant environment as You were on that subway in New York." By the grace of God I was brought up short to realize that, as helpful as the environment was, it was no substitute for personal, firsthand contact with the living God.

Spiritual Reality in Giving Away Your Life

We have already said that collapse in the Christian life is never a blowout—it is always a slow leak. That's true. Samson is a precise example of this. He "knew not that the Lord had departed from him." A wonderful home background can never substitute for a bona fide life with the Lord Jesus Christ. Let's guard against the mistake of becoming environmental Christians, depending for spiritual sustenance on surrounding conditions rather than on firsthand, personal contact with the living God. We can have firsthand data in the Christian life. This comes from unconditionally giving away our lives to the Lord.

[illegible]

5

THE PRESENCE OF GOD IN GIVING AWAY YOUR LIFE

Another Old Testament statement that gives us a clue about spiritual reality is found in Exodus 34:29: "When Moses came down from Mount Sinai, with the two tables of testimony in his hand as he came down from the mountain, Moses did not know that the skin of his face shone because he had been talking with God."

Think how Moses' unawareness differed from Samson's. What a contrast! Samson did not know that the Lord had departed from him; Moses did not know that his face shone with the Lord's glory!

When you have spiritual reality, when you've been in the presence of God, you don't have to wear a sign saying, "Look how spiritual I am!" The more one makes remarks to let people know how spiritual he is (in case they didn't catch it!), the more his words show that he probably does not have the reality he's talking about. But *Moses was a man who really lived in the presence of God.* That's how he got to the place where his face shone without his knowing it. There is no other way to acquire that shine.

The Glory of the Lord

How do we go about such a life? We go about it as we

take seriously the fact that the Lord Jesus Christ is alive, that the Holy Spirit is an active personal Agent, and that the Word of God is the living and powerful place in which we see God Himself. Paul says in 2 Corinthians 3:18, "We all, with unveiled face, *beholding the glory of the Lord*, are being changed into his likeness from one degree of glory to another; for this comes from the Lord, who is the Spirit."

There is absolutely no substitute for being personally in the presence of God alone. We could have special church services every week of the year, but that would still not substitute for the need of every one of us to enter personally into the presence of God every day. It was only because Moses was *personally in God's presence* that his face shone without his realizing it.

I can hear you saying, "Don't tell me you're suggesting a legalistic practice—that I've got to spend an allotted amount of time each day with God!" No, that's not what I'm suggesting. There is a vast difference between bondage and discipline. Legalistic bondage is something hateful. A legalistic practice is something we have to do and we don't want to! Ugh! But discipline is something else.

Discipline Transforms

Unlike legalistic bondage, discipline is something that completely transforms us because it is an attitude we take voluntarily. We may not feel all revved up at the moment, but in our heart of hearts we have made a decision of the will that we will want to meet with God daily. We meet Him day by day because we realize the phenomenal fact that He wants to meet with us!

I hope this thought fully grips you. It is not just a question of our meeting with the living God. The phenomenal fact is that the Creator of the universe desires an interview with us every day so He can have our fellowship and our worship daily!

"The Father seeks such to worship Him," our Lord said

in John 4:23. I'm left speechless at the thought! If we are failing to meet alone, personally and regularly with the living God, we are robbing God of something He longs for. It is hard to comprehend how the Creator of the universe could want to meet with us, but the awesome and glorious fact is that He does. For this reason the primary question is not, "What do I get out of my quiet time and of my personal fellowship with God?" but "What does God get out of my fellowship with Him?" By the grace of God I get a great deal out of those times. But that's not the prime issue. The real point is that I meet with the living God because I love Him. This takes it out of the realm of legalism entirely.

No Falling Stars

Sometimes when Christians teach about personal fellowship with God, they present the idea almost as though the stars are going to fall out of heaven and you'll flunk all your exams or have an automobile accident if you miss a quiet time. Of course this is foolish. You can skip a meal or two of physical food. No problem. In fact, it's probably good for you now and then. But you wouldn't want to skip often.

You see, your quiet times are not a rigid thing. It may be that in a given situation it is not possible for you to meet with the Lord Jesus. But how are you going to feel physically if you go for six weeks with just one big fat meal each Sunday and a little snack on Wednesday night? How's your physical health going to be? You're going to be in pretty sad shape. That kind of starvation will beat Metrecal in taking off weight, but it will take a few other things off, too! The same is true in the spiritual realm.

Although meeting with God is not a rigid, legalistic thing, suppose you go for weeks without personally coming to the Lord and having Him speak to you through His Word. How do you think you're going to be in terms of spiritual power and spiritual tone? You'll be anemic. Even though you may have had the privilege of hearing a lot of fine preaching, the need for direct contact with the Lord Jesus Christ is not eliminated.

"I Don't Feel Like It"

You may be saying, "But I don't feel like it. If I were really a victorious Christian, each morning I would feel like leaping up and rushing right to my desk and taking my Bible." Sound familiar? In this connection I have read some comforting words by George Mueller, a man of God who knew God well and who through prayer and the grace of God was able to support dozens of orphanages in Great Britain. Mueller's unforgettable little tract on personal devotions contains a sentence that has been a special comfort to me. He said: "I feel that it is my greatest responsibility before God and man to get my soul happy before the Lord before I face anybody." The expression which speaks to me is "get my soul happy." That implies that when George Mueller woke up he felt just like I do—like cold mashed potatoes! He didn't swing from the rafters with delight any more than you or I do. He realized that it was his responsibility before God to get hold of himself and get into the presence of God in order to get his soul happy in the Lord.

This is one of the reasons why God wants us to meet with Him. He knows we need Him. It is as we meditate on Him and on His will and on His Word and on the wonder of who He is, that our souls get happy before the Lord. As we remind ourselves day by day of all that the Lord Jesus Christ has done for us, and of all that He is, we get out of the doldrums.

Where Would I Be?

Sometimes when I'm feeling miserable I sit down for ten or fifteen minutes and try to answer the question, "Where would I be today if the Lord Jesus Christ had never come into my life?" Often I find myself singing inwardly after that short meditation break, even though I might really have been dragging anchor before that time. This is what God intends to happen in personal fellowship with Him. When was the last time you got something directly from the Word of God through the Holy Spirit, apart from reinforcement from someone else? If it's been a long time, may I recommend that you read some Scriptures and try it!

Prayer is a vital aspect of fellowship with God. When our spirits are in the presence of God in prayer our faces will shine. One Sunday Alexander Whyte, the Great Scottish preacher, preached a tremendous message. After the sermon someone said to him, "You preached as though you had just come from the presence of the Lord." With a faraway look in his eye he said, "Perhaps I did."

This should be the experience of every one of us—that we come from the presence of God. But again, this is not easy. The statement, "I don't feel like praying" is perfectly natural. The Enemy will do everything within his power to keep you and me from our knees. Five thousand legitimate things can keep us from the presence of God—an exam, a letter that has to be written, somebody knocking on our door, the phone ringing, the baby crying. Almost anything can keep us from the presence of God. So we need to work hard at keeping in touch with God. For it's profoundly true that Satan trembles when he sees the weakest believer on his knees. It is there that spiritual victories are won.

Whipped in the Battle

I was tremendously encouraged several years ago when I was privileged to be in England at a great Keswick convention. There I heard John R. W. Stott give an address to ministers on ministerial priorities. Speaking of prayer, Stott said something that I think I will never forget. He said: "You know, brethren, I find a strange paradox in my life. I find that the thing which I know gives me the deepest joy and the deepest pleasure, namely, to be in the presence of God unhurried, is the thing that I find I least want to do." Then he added, "I find I must fight continually what I call the battle of the threshold. The Enemy will keep us by every means, fair or foul, from breaking through and taking that time. And if we are whipped there, we are whipped."

Moses, in the presence of God, did not know that his face shone. You and I are in the presence of God as we read and meditate in His Word, as we spend time in prayer, taking God seriously. He is the only One who counts. In His presence we engage not only in prayers of appeal to God, but in other dimensions of prayer too. For example, worship and thankfulness. Have you ever taken fifteen minutes alone with the Lord without requesting one single thing? Try it sometime. It's amazing how saying "thank you" and worshiping and adoring the Lord lifts up your own soul in strength.

Tell Him You Love Him

I remember Dr. Jack Mitchell of Dallas Theological Seminary telling about a student who came to him and said, "Dr. Mitchell, I don't understand what's wrong with me. I came in here on fire for the Lord, but somehow in three years I've lost the enthusiasm I had when I first came." (I hope this hasn't happened to you, but it very easily can.) Dr. Mitchell responded, "Let me ask you one question. When was the last time you told the Lord Jesus Christ you loved Him?" The fellow looked at him oddly and said, "Well, you mean, uh, what do you mean? He knows I love Him. I'm knocking myself out for Him in my Christian service assignments and all kinds of other things. He knows I love Him. What do you mean 'tell Him'?"

Dr. Mitchell persisted with his question, "What I asked you was, when was the last time you told Him you loved Him?" "Well," the student admitted, "it's been quite a while." Dr. Mitchell replied, "I suggest you go back and do it."

The next day the fellow came back to Dr. Mitchell and said, "It's astounding! My whole spiritual life has been revolutionized, and I feel I'm back in fellowship with the Lord in a way I haven't been for years!" He had gotten into this situation simply by being absorbed in *doing* things for the Lord, He had failed to realize that first of all the Lord wanted *him* personally—wanted his worship and his adoration.

In all honesty, any of us can make the mistake this student made. When was the last time you told the Lord you loved Him? Now again when you say you love the Lord you will not have the same kind of sentimental feeling you have when you say you love your spouse or your fiance or your current heartthrob. That's not the kind of love we're talking about. It's not some kind of ooey, gooey, soupy feeling; it's a moving, virile thing—a desire to obey.

The Obedience of Love

How did our Lord define love? In John 14:21 He says, "He who has my commandments and keeps them, he it is who loves me." It's not "he who tells me in a quavery voice he loves me," but "he who *has my commandments and keeps them*." That's the acid test of whether we love our Lord. Not how we feel internally (although obviously there will be an element of emotion involved), but whether we are prepared to really follow the Lord Jesus Christ in obedience.

The same principle, incidentally, applies to loving your neighbor. Sometimes students have said to me, "You know, I don't really love that fellow next door like I love my girl. There must be something wrong with me." Let me suggest what C. S. Lewis has pointed out—that the Scriptures say we are to love the Lord our God with all our heart, soul, strength, and mind, and our neighbors as ourselves.

How do you love yourself? When you look in the mirror you don't swoon. (At least I hope you don't. If you do there's something wrong!) The way I love myself is that I want the best for me, myself, and I. And how do you love your neighbor as yourself? By wanting the best for your neighbor. It's not because you have an emotional, gooey feeling about him. And how do we love our Lord? By wanting Him first and putting Him first in every area of our lives, by giving Him everything we have and are, and by doing what He wants us to do. That's the test of our love for the Lord Jesus Christ.

Prime the Pump

This kind of commitment is the starting point for cultivating the presence of God in all its dimensions. If you sometimes have difficulty knowing how to begin, and you feel like the cold mashed potatoes I mentioned, take your hymnbook and share in the spiritual experience of some of the great men of God. For example, take the hymn, "And can it be that I should gain an interest in the Saviour's blood?" Follow along in the footsteps of these men who had better gifts of expression than you and I do. Draw out your "heart of stone" in response to the Lord and say, "Yes, Lord, that's exactly what I feel, only I can't express it as well!" Prime the pump by this method, and you'll find yourself rejoicing in the presence of God.

There's a kind of reverent hilarity in God's presence. It is "joy unspeakable and full of glory" as expressed by Paul. Moses was awed by the "greatness of God's excellence." He described the Lord as "my strength and my song." Jeremiah proclaimed his Redeemer as "strong." Isaiah "mentioned" the multitude of the loving kindnesses of the Lord, His goodness and His compassion. The angel of God's presence saved him. His love and mercy redeemed Him. God lifted him and carried him all the days of old (Isaiah 63:7-9).

When David found conspiracies coming against him he hid in the secret of God's presence. Under a barrage of gossip, he fled to God's secret shelter (Psalm 31:20). He then describes God's presence as "fullness of joy and pleasures forevermore" (Psalm 16:11).

The strength and joy of God's presence comes because He is not remote or unreachable. God actually lifted His people and carried them. And He so identified with them that in their affliction God, too was afflicted (Isaiah 63:9). Beyond my comprehension!

This experience is the exact opposite of the facade put on by the religious leaders of Christ's day. He denounced them for drawing near to God with their lips, but their hearts were far, far from genuine love for Him. By contrast, true love for the Lord is described in Psalm 84:5 as possessed by "those in whose hearts are the highways to Zion."

Could you describe your heart as grooved with the highways to Zion?

The Help We Need

The practice of God's presence, the discipline of heart-communion with Him can only be done because we deeply sense our need for Him. We know it is impossible to become a Christian without Jesus Christ and His death for us. It is equally impossible to live the Christian life by our own expertise and abilities. Someone has said it's like standing in a bathtub and trying to get out by raising your two feet off the bottom at the same time. We need help.

The incredible thing is that God has already given you and me everything we will ever get in terms of the potentiality of living the Christian life. "Oh," you say, "that can't be. If I stop here I'm really in bad shape—I have a long way to go. Surely God has more for me than He has given me now." He *does* have more for you in the experiential development of what He has given, but you already have everything you need for the Christian life, for He has given you the Lord Jesus Christ Himself.

Turn with me to 2 Peter 1:2-3 for a summary statement of tremendous fact. "May grace and peace be multiplied unto you in the knowledge of God and of Jesus our Lord. His divine power has granted to us all things that pertain to life and godliness through the knowledge of Him who called us to His own glory and excellence." This is what God has given you and me in the Lord Jesus Christ—everything that is necessary for a life of holiness and godliness.

If you are like me, you know you were not immediately and totally perfect in thought, word and deed after you became a Christian. A change in motivation and attitude took place but not instant perfection. If this happened, we would immediately lose any need for staying in God's presence or depending on Him. We might even be foolish enough to think that our good life was all our own virtue and merit. We would become intolerably proud. And there is nothing that reeks more in the nostrils of God than spiritual pride.

Spiritual Pride

The web of spiritual pride is one of those subtle snares that entangles us without warning. If God has blessed you in your Christian life, guard against self-congratulation. We could be in the most mortal danger spiritually just after we have had a tremendous meeting with God. It is then we are tempted to think of ourselves more highly than we ought to think as we look around at other people who may not have had the same exhilarating experience or seen the same truths which God has shown us. If we fall into that vicious trap, the Enemy will divert our attention to ourselves. Instantly we are cut off from Divine power and blessing and paralysis sets in.

How Does It Work for Me?

"Well," you say, "how does this become an every day experience for me? You've made a very nice statement, and it's wonderful and I know it's true. How does it actually work for me at 10:30 A.M. on Tuesday when I'm about to take up that old habit again? How does it become meaningful to me at 5:30 P.M. when I find myself ready to give in to a temptation? How do I come to know spiritual reality? I hear that term a lot and it sounds wonderful, but there are no bells ringing in my head. How do I know when I've got spiritual reality?"

At this point you must know what you are looking for. When I talk to non-Christians or agnostics, they frequently say, "I would believe in God if He could be proven to me." But when you ask them what they would accept as proof, they're at a loss to tell you. They actually don't know what kind of proof they're looking for, and consequently they never find it. Christians have a similar problem. We're concerned about the truths we hear taught but don't always understand the application to our lives. We're not quite sure what we should be looking for. We hear someone say that God spoke to him or her, and we think to ourselves, "Well, I never heard God speak to me. I must not be on as high a spiritual level as that person."

We cannot duplicate someone else's spiritual experience. The Lord Jesus Christ will meet each of us where we are, according to our own need. It may or may not parallel somebody else's experience in terms of its outworking. But we *will know* when the Lord Jesus Christ has met with us and we *will know* the reality that He alone can give.

Let's suppose you're ready to blow your fuse. Your patience has been tried to the breaking point. It's not natural to be patient in that situation; it's supernatural. At that moment, consciously and by faith, ask for the presence and power of the Lord Jesus Christ. Then thank Him for delivering you.

At the point of testing, we can turn our minds consciously to the Lord Jesus Christ. He is a living Person today. He is not just a series of fixed facts on a piece of paper. He is a dynamic Personality who, though invisible, is intensely real—more real than this book in your hands. Because He is alive we will find Him beginning to release His attitudes and attributes within us. This is the glory of the Christian life. It is supernatural. Responsiveness to His presence makes giving away our lives a deep and exciting experience of maturation!

6

PURITY AND PEACE IN GIVING AWAY YOUR LIFE

In 25 years of staff work with Inter-Varsity Christian Fellowship our summers, holidays, Christmases were regularly spent, not at home, but at student camps. It had many advantages. At eight months of age our daughter had been in eight states!

From all of the many camps stretching from California to Ontario, Canada one conversation my wife and I had with a student stands out in my memory, perhaps because we were up half the night. It was with a student named Connie from Florida and was a heavy, emotional talk in which Connie cried and confessed and prayed and cried again. The anguish of this graduating student kept us awake even after we had gone to our room. She had poured out her heart in utter agony. She was tempted and harassed by impure thoughts and was in constant struggle. She was certain she would get worse, if it continued.

Connie was an extremely capable girl and seemed to be deeply spiritual. She had applied to go to the mission field and few of the students in the IVCF group equaled her energy. While carrying a full load at the university she took correspondence courses in Bible subjects. She could always be counted on for any of the IVCF activities as well. That night we asked the Lord Jesus to deliver her and prayed long and earnestly. Exhausted physically and emotionally, we continued to feel the weight of her burden.

The next morning at breakfast, still not quite awake, I was jolted to look across the room to see a bright-eyed, laughing Connie. She was beaming from ear to ear. As soon as we could see her alone, she brimmed over with confidence and joy. "The Lord has delivered me, I know" were her words. It was such a different Connie. Well, we had prayed, hadn't we? The Lord had answered! She went on to spend a number of fruitful years in South America as a missionary.

Anyone can be tempted in the area of purity. We can cry, "Lord, I don't have the purity of mind that I need. At times, I find myself being overcome by temptation. Is there any way out?" Then we remember those tremendous words in 1 Corinthians 10:13: "No temptation has overtaken you that is not common to man. God is faithful and he will not allow you to be tempted beyond your strength, but with the temptation will provide the way of escape, that you may be able to endure it."

I believe we're heading into an age (and are already in an age, in fact) when we're going to be more sorely tempted in this area of purity than at almost any other time in history since the first century of Christianity. We're moving back toward the mores and practices of the pagan society of Corinth. Even the secularists are telling us this. Dr. Pitirim A. Sorokin, the noted Harvard sociologist, wrote a book titled *The Crisis of Our Age*, and this is the very point that he discusses—our impure, sex-mad society is headed toward decline. And so far as I know, Dr. Sorokin does not claim to be a Christian.

Deliverance from Temptation

How does the reality of the Lord Jesus Christ become meaningful to us in recurring temptations? In the first place, be realistic about temptations to impurity. God's promise that we will be able to withstand the temptation actually *precedes* the temptation. We know in advance there are certain places, certain times, certain people, certain kinds of literature that tempt us. God does not promise to deliver us if we deliberately walk into the teeth of that temptation when, by His grace, before the fact we could have avoided the situation. We need to be realistic, we need to be ruthless with ourselves, eliminating activities or contacts that bring us close to temptation.

At other times we are taken by temptation unawares. In those situations, how can we react and find the power of Christ in our lives? The secret is to transfer our thoughts to the Lord Jesus Himself.

We can make the mistake, particularly in the area of impurity of thought, of trying to fight the thought itself. The more we fight it, the worse it gets. Many of our thoughts are involuntary and come in unawares. They pop up into our heads and even frighten and disturb us that they are there. We ask, "Lord, how could this be if I'm a Christian? How could this thought be here?" When a thought comes into our minds involuntarily, that in itself is not sin. It's what we do with the thought and what action we take when we recognize the wrong thought, that determines whether we overcome or fall into sin.

The Nature of the Thought Life

To illustrate the involuntary nature of the thought life, and how we try to fight the thought itself instead of transferring the problem to the Lord Jesus Christ, suppose I say to you, "Don't think of white elephants for the next ten minutes. Now don't think of white elephants. Remember, don't think of white elephants!" Well, the more you try not to think of white elephants, the more you think of white elephants! The only way to beat the white elephants, and the only way to beat temptation, is to transfer your attention, to something else.

The moment we are aware of a thought in our hearts and minds that is unworthy of the Lord Jesus Christ, whether it involves impurity or some other kind of wrong thought, we need to immediately and consciously turn to the Lord Jesus Christ by faith and say, "Lord, it's Your purity I need, Your promise to deliver. By faith I lay hold of this. I lay hold of You because You are living in me."

"Christ in you, the hope of glory," Paul says. The power of the Holy Spirit will drive out every wrong thought. In this way, *He* and *we* can bring every thought into the captivity to Christ.

The Common Temptations

Let me also say this about temptation. It's not uncommon to feel, "I'm the only person in the world who's got a problem. If I were really spiritual I wouldn't be tempted like this. I would always be completely pure." But remember, Paul said our temptations are common to man.

One crying need in the church of the Lord Jesus Christ is to develop honesty with one another. We need to drop our masks and share with each other with uncontrived openness. Then we can draw on the resources of the Lord Jesus together. Instead of putting up a front and appearing to be completely perfect, we can support each other. We can pray for each other and experience God's deliverance through agreeing prayer. It is true, everyone has similar temptations.

One common problem is an inability to love one particular unlovely person. What do we do in such a situation? It may be completely unnatural for us to love that person—it may seem impossible! On a natural plane we cannot drum up love. But by faith we can turn to the Lord Jesus and say, "Lord, it's Your love that must be shed abroad in my heart. I don't have this love; I confess that I do not have this love; my natural reaction is to despise this person. As You release Your love in my life I will be able to love him in the power of Your Holy Spirit." The more we realize that the power and the reality is in Christ rather than in ourselves, the easier it is to stay humble.

Peace in Christ

The glory of the Christian life is that in Christ we have peace and contentment, even though every conceivable circumstance around us would lead us to restlessness and lack of peace. How do we come to peace in Christ? It is not by trying to whip up peace: "I've got to be peaceful, I've got to be peaceful, I've got to be peaceful. I'm going to be pure today. I'm not going to get knocked down today. Impatience! Boy, you watch me, and I'm going to be self control personified!" That's the way a lot of us try to live the Christian life, isn't it?

Trying to live the Christian life without the Lord Jesus Christ, as Ian Thomas says, is like trying to push an automobile up a hill. It's impossible. We get defeated every time. But in Christ we say, "Lord, it's Your peace that I need, the peace that passes understanding, that is unnatural, that is supernatural. I ask you by faith, to release your peace in my life."

To have joy and peace when a loved one dies is not natural. There is a certain sense in which we Christians sorrow, but we do not sorrow as those who have no hope or faith. It is by faith in the Lord Jesus Christ, as He releases His peace in our lives, that we are able to rest in Him. Only the grace of Christ enables us to do this.

The Faithful One

This principle of concentrating not on our own faith but on the Faithful One, the object of our faith, is the great secret that Hudson Taylor learned. If you've never read *Hudson Taylor's Spiritual Secret,* go to a Christian bookstore and pick up a copy. It's been a tremendous help to thousands and thousands of Christians over the years. When Hudson Taylor was in China he found himself in a desperate struggle, increasingly bogged down in the quicksand of self-effort. Finally a letter from a friend had a phrase in it that gave Taylor the shaft of light he needed. It opened the window that revolutionized him.

His friend pointed out to him that the secret to faith is not concentrating on one's own faith ("I've got to have more faith"), but to look away to the Faithful One. As Hudson Taylor understood something of the experiential reality of this, he came into a new joy and a new experience of the Lord. We speak of "great people of God," but it's not so much "great people of God" as it is people with a great God. We don't make God any bigger by our believing in Him, but we get bigger ourselves as we get a vision of Him. It is as we understand Him the way He really is, that we are able to live in faith and power and confidence.

Your God Is Too Small

J. B. Phillips wrote the apt book *Your God Is Too Small*, and I'm afraid the title expresses a truth about many of us. We have such a limited vision of God and who He is.

Both the Old and New Testaments are replete with accounts of men who were ordinary human beings. The Bible does not gloss over their weaknesses. The eleventh chapter of Hebrews lists some of them. In each case, the vignettes describing their lives are begun by the two words, "by faith." Those "heroes of faith" simply looked beyond the earthly facts to their all-wise, all-powerful God, and to His promises. Even in logic-defying circumstances they knew He was adequate.

In our own time the real test of faith for many of us as Christians is not so much whether God exists but whether God is good. In the goodness of God we are able to live, as someone has said, not somehow but triumphantly. When we are assured of His goodness He enables us to transcend all the events and circumstances of life, whether they be pain or joy or death or suffering.

The Shield of Faith

Let's return to Romans 8:32: "He who did not spare his own Son but gave him up for us all, will he not also give us all things with him?" This is the faith, the shield, of which Paul speaks in Ephesians 6:16—the shield "with which you can quench all the flaming darts of the evil one." When we grasp this shield of faith in the Lord Jesus Christ, and see the fact of His love demonstrated on the Cross, we are able to respond triumphantly to the tragic circumstances of any given moment. This is the key to reality in this area. It's a tremendous thing to know by faith that our lives are in God's hands. He enables us to live joyfully in the present and full of hope for the future.

Anxiety is another thing which can make us miserable and destroy our Christian growth. The tendency is to label this attitude as a personality weakness rather than call it a sin. The love of the Lord Jesus Christ for us and His total truthfulness to us takes the worry out of the future. He commands us to give our cares and anxieties to Him.

I do a lot of flying, and it seems that just when I'm ready to leave on a trip, I hear of a plane crash somewhere. It's not a great comfort to me or to my wife and family, believe me! If I didn't believe by faith that my life was in the hand of God, I would never get on an airplane. (But remember, statistics show that more people die in bed than anywhere else!) The point is that faith enables us to enter into life confidently and triumphantly.

Faith Versus Fatalism

"Well," you say, "what's the difference between what you're describing and a fatalistic outlook on life?" All the difference in the world. A fatalistic outlook is nothing but a trust in a blind, impersonal, inexorable force. But faith in God is confidence in the sovereign action of a God who loves us as a Father loves His children. "As a father pities his children, so the Lord loves those who trust Him." We know that as God works out the circumstances of our lives, it is the working of a loving Father.

It's not God's practice to ask us to understand—He only asks us to trust Him. There are many things in life that you and I cannot understand. "Why did God allow this tragedy to happen? Why did God take this person when He did?" We cannot understand, and God doesn't ask us to understand—He only asks us to trust Him.

Suppose you have a little child in a room where sharp knives are in reach so that he could hurt himself. He's playing and having a great time, but you quickly grab him and put him in another room. He's very unhappy because he thinks you're destroying his pleasure in taking him away from such nice toys. As a parent you don't ask him to understand—you just ask him to trust you. That's exactly what God asks us to do in all of the events of life.

Faith and Action

Faith, then, is the key to experiential reality in the Christian life. Faith lays hold of the givens and lives accordingly. It cannot be a dead thing. Faith, if it is genuine, will always lead us to action. The New Testament definition of faith is "that which demands action on the basis of what is being believed."

Suppose someone comes into my house who looks half-crazed and inebriated and says, "I put a bomb under your house and it's going off in ten minutes." If I say I believe it, there's a very simple way to test whether I really believe it, and that's to see whether I'm still at home ten minutes later. If I'm still there, and I say I believe the drunkard, I'm really not being honest.

And if we say we believe that the Lord Jesus Christ is the Savior of the world, and that without Him men are lost, without hope, without God and that in Christ alone is the answer to life and eternity, yet we just sit around and do nothing about it, who are we kidding? We are certainly not kidding the non-Christians observing us, and probably not the other Christians either; we are only kidding ourselves.

Genuine faith is active and dynamic in the Christian life at every level. The secret is that we have the Lord Jesus Christ to lead us, to support us and guide us. We need only to realize the profound truth that the Lord Jesus Christ is the Source of reality for day-by-day living as well as for salvation itself.

Total Commitment

What is it to be filled with the Holy Spirit? What is it to have a Spirit-filled life? I believe that in many respects we've made the Christian life unduly complicated. I've read everything I could get my hands on about the victorious life and the filling of the Holy Spirit, because I want all of God there is to get. But I believe the essence is very simple. It is basically *total commitment to the* Lord Jesus Christ, without reservation, for every area of our lives and for every moment we live as far as we know our own hearts. This means that day by day we give every part of our being to Him, every detail of life, every event that comes to us, every response and reaction we feel, we commit to Him. Nothing can be withheld. In total faith in Him we rest in His care.

Let me make one more observation. You may be saying, nervously, "Maybe there's some sin in my life that I don't see, and maybe this is a problem." Stop worrying. I think a lot of us drive ourselves out of our minds unnecessarily because we don't understand the character of God. We need only pray the prayer that David prayed in Psalm 139:23-24, "Search me, O God, and know my heart! Try me and know my thoughts! And see if there be any wicked way in me, and lead me in the way everlasting." God will show us our needs. Let us not assume that there must be some hidden cancer that He hasn't shown us that is causing a spiritual short-circuit.

7

DYNAMIC RESULTS IN GIVING AWAY YOUR LIFE

We can't test how much we love the Lord Jesus Christ by feeling our pulses or checking the amount of quaver in our voices when we speak about Him. There is, however, a very simple test of our love for Him. Our Lord said it: "He who has my commandments and keeps them, he it is who loves me" (John 14:21).

The test of our love, then, is not what we say or even how we feel, but what we do. The Lord gives each of us the privilege of serving Him and obeying His commandments. He expects results in our lives, dynamic results. He could take us home to heaven the moment we become Christians, but He does not. Instead, He gives us the exciting adventure of serving Him for a while on earth.

The right attitude in giving away our lives to Christ is epitomized by the experience of the Apostle Paul on the road to Damascus. Paul was on his way to Damascus for the sole purpose of persecuting the church. On the way, he was struck down by a blinding light and heard a voice from Heaven. As soon as he realized who was speaking, he fell down and said, "Lord, what wilt thou have me to do?" (Acts 9:6 *KJV*). That was his first step in serving Jesus Christ effectively. He came as a servant. He reported for duty and asked His Lord for an assignment.

Sometimes we have an attitude that looks very spiritual. On the surface it differs so little from what we have just seen Paul do that the distinction is often passed over unnoticed. But the real difference is this: *we* do the deciding. *We* elect what we are going to do. Then we say, "Lord, I'm going to do this or that for You. I've got it all mapped out."

This is not God's plan for service to Him. He says we are to come to Him and say, "Lord, what will *You* have me to do?" This acknowledges *Him* as the Commander-in-Chief. He knows the whole, all the aspects of where the need is. He also knows our capabilities better than we do. And if we let Him, He will assign us to that place where we will fit hand-in-glove.

The beginning, then, is to check our attitude toward serving Him. Are we deciding what we're going to do for Him or are we asking Him, "Lord, what do *You* want me to do?"

No Games with God

God doesn't play games with us. If we are honest with Him, he's honest with us. He wants us to walk in joyful day-by-day fellowship with Him. Variety will come to our personal experiences. None of us lives every minute on a super-high peak of emotion. We couldn't possibly continue at the same peak of feeling that we have at the end of a basketball game with thirteen seconds to go and the other team in possession of the ball! We would go mad. Emotions are undulant. We needn't feel badly if we're not turning cartwheels every moment. If we understand the principle of faith in the Christian life, and that Christ is the object of that faith, we will experience the constancy that comes from a life truly given away to Him.

I want to quote a hymn that means a great deal to me. It expresses the whole spectrum of experience in the Christian life and touches on the very thing we've been talking about.

I take thy promise, Lord, in all its length and breadth and fullness as my daily strength. Into life's future fearless I may gaze, for Jesus, Thou art with me all the days.

There may be days of darkness and distress, when sin has power to tempt and care to press. Yet in the darkest day I will not fear, for amid the shadows Thou wilt still be near.

Days there may be of joy and deep delight, when earth seems fairest and her skies most bright; then draw me closer to Thee, lest I rest elsewhere, my Savior, than upon Thy breast.

And all the other days that make my life, marked by no special joy or grief or strife, days filled with quiet duties, trivial care, burdens too small for other hearts to share—

Spend Thou these days with me. All shall be Thine, so shall the darkest hour with glory shine. Then, when these earthly years have passed away, let me be with Thee in the perfect day.

—H. L. R. Deck

Do You Want the Light of God in Your Face?

Now, this service for Christ is no ordinary service. Nor is it an odious task we must put up with because it's part of the price tag of Christianity. Far from it! It means working for the King of Kings and the Most High God. It is the greatest privilege any human being could ever have. The Lord invites His people to invest their lives in work that will last for all eternity, to be co-workers with Him, in the power of the Holy Spirit. Nothing compares with it.

King David said, "Serve the Lord with gladness" (Psalm 100:2). Have you known people serving the Lord Jesus Christ but somehow you felt sorry for them because they seemed anything but glad, only burdened and overwhelmed? You may have found yourself thinking, "Boy, I hope I never have to do what they're doing." Well, strange to say, some Christians do work with that hang-dog attitude. On the other hand, we've all seen those who've had the very light of God shining in their faces. Obviously, they find their work sheer joy. Even in hard places their enthusiasm is undiluted. They've found the secret of serving Jesus Christ with joy. They've responded in love to the one who loved them first.

Our Lord said, "My yoke is easy and my burden is light" (Matthew 11:30). Can a yoke be easy? Or a burden light? It can if it is a yoke of service in love.

Christians have established, perhaps unconsciously, a hierarchy of values in Christian service that is not found in Christ's teaching. No one gets three more spiritual Brownie points for being in Africa than for being in Chicago. Nor are there more merit points for being in the "full-time ministry" than for being a truly Christian automobile mechanic. The question is, what job does God's plan take us into? In any honorable vocation we can glorify God. He needs workers everywhere. In every occupation there is opportunity to minister to the people around us. Paul points out that this is possible with an extreme example in Ephesians. "Slaves," he says, "be obedient to those who are your earthly masters, with fear and trembling, in singleness of heart, as to Christ; not in the ways of eyeservice, as men pleasers, but as servants of Christ doing the will of God from the heart" (Ephesians 6:5-6).

Our Daily Occupation

It follows, then, that in our daily occupation to which God has called us, we work not merely to earn money to pay our bills, but also to honor Jesus Christ. When we do the job to His glory, we are investing our lives for Him. A college student who also works part time at a lunch counter can honor God in each place. People who do secular work all day and take on additional work in the church or in a parachurch organization can likewise serve Him in both kinds of work.

In fact, when properly understood, there is no division between sacred and secular in the life of a Christian. All that I am and all that I have belongs to the Lord Jesus Christ. My very breath and energy belong to Him. The whole of my life is lived out as His servant. I wash dishes to the glory of God. I jog to the glory of God. I explore the Bible, pray, and witness to the glory of God. Everything is part of a life given to the Lord Jesus Christ. It is the same for all people who have given themselves unreservedly to the Lord.

This is a liberating concept of Christian service. And the freedom is real, not imagined, because the results of each day's work come from His hand. When our projected plans go awry, He may have a lesson to teach us. When schedules are reversed, leaving us helplessly restricted, He may be nudging us in a different direction. When interruptions come by phone or doorbell, we can make the necessary adjustments in our work. When the car breaks down or the plane is late, our spirits can be at peace. For He is in charge of each moment, each event of every day. At the day's end, we just thank Him for whatever He brought us during that day. That's the way it works.

For the remainder of this chapter we shall consider some varieties of service that can be adapted to almost anyone's situation.

"Nursery Classes"

A few years ago I visited All Souls Church in London, the church pastored by Dr. John R. W. Stott. He ran a continuing cycle of thirteen weeks of training classes called "nursery classes." Every new believer who comes into the church goes through that cycle to discover the basics of the Christian life. In some churches there is no such mechanism to help beginners. As a matter of fact, practical, applied instruction is somewhat of a new trend. It seems to me that every church should offer some foundational courses for everyone entering the church. The minimum should include the basic principles for living as a Christian and then graduate to simple doctrinal courses and from there go to overall Biblical content. Elective courses are another option. The possibilities are endless. But a planned strategy is important.

In connection with church plans, open bookstores, lending libraries and tape libraries. Make it easy for the people to obtain materials and urge their use. I've met some groups where tape-listening classes are common. A tape series will be selected and each week the group will listen together and then discuss the content.

Neighborhood Bible Studies

An important method of outreach is neighborhood Bible study. This kind of study can be held either in a home or in a church. I used to think you couldn't hold such studies in a church building, but more recently I've decided that you can if you don't apologize for it. Of course, some people won't come because it is in a church building, but others *will* come.

One thing we discovered at Arlington Countryside Chapel is that if neighborhood Bible studies are held in the church building, people are much more likely to hang in at your church. If a person comes to Christ at a home study, it's harder for them to establish a relationship with the local fellowship. For example, ninety or a hundred women come to our Wednesday morning studies. They are divided into groups of eight or ten each. Over a period of time a number of people have come to the Lord and have become part of the fellowship at our church.

Now here are several important things to keep in mind if you're going to have successful evangelistic Bible studies. First, *you've got to have a majority or at least an equal number of non-Christians.* Ten Christians studying John 3:16 is not an evangelistic Bible study! This obvious fact has apparently escaped a number of people. They don't understand why they don't get converts when they go fishing in the bathtub! You've got to have non-Christians. You can be studying the color of the Beast's eyes in Revelation with ten *believers*, but you are much more likely to see conversions when you're studying John 3:16 with ten *unbelievers*!

If the non-Christians are in the majority, a more relaxed atmosphere develops. When the non-Christians are in the *minority*, they feel like targets rather than participants. But how do you guarantee a majority of non-Christians? It's very simple. Limit the number of Christians per class! Begin with three or four or five per class—no more. If you've got a total of twenty Christians, start five groups with four Christians each. Shoot for a *total* of twelve to sixteen people per group, with Christians limited to a minority. How do you get started? Go out and canvass—with enthusiasm, not apology— and invite people to come.

No Skin Off Your Nose

When it comes to witnessing and inviting people to a meeting or a Bible study, most of us are like Elmer Blurt, the old radio salesman. He used to go up and knock on a door and say to himself, "Nobody home, I hope, I hope, I hope." That's the way we are. We approach people, "Y-y-you're not interested in spiritual things, oh well, just in case you are, I thought, oh, you're not interested, I know." Never apologize for extending the invitation. Say, instead, "If you'd like to come, you'd enjoy it."

A begging approach will turn people off. We've got to move out and tell them, "Listen, have you heard? At ten o'clock on Wednesday morning a number of us are getting together to study the New Testament and how it relates to life. It's a great thing, and we'd like to have you come." Show that it's no skin off your nose if they don't come, that you're doing him or her a favor by inviting them. Enthusiasm with warmth makes the best invitation.

If you stop to think about it, that is indeed the case! If a person comes to know Christ, you're doing him the greatest favor in his life. You have come to his door and told him about an opportunity to know the Lord of life. You don't have to apologize for that. It's the greatest thing that can ever happen to a person. If we can once drop our apologetic mentality and get away from being afraid of our own shadow, we're going to find a much greater response than is otherwise possible.

A Means to the End

It's important to realize that Bible study discussions are not an end in themselves, but simply a means to an end. Usually a person does not come to Christ in the study; almost invariably it happens when one of the Christians has the person over for coffee afterwards, or at some other time during the week, and says, "Well, what do you think?" and then fills in the gospel systematically.

You know, you can't get John 3:16 out of every verse in the Gospel of Mark. If you force each paragraph to teach salvation, the whole thing gets so hokeyed up and artificial that the non-Christian realizes he is being singled out as a target and may back out of the whole thing. The book of Mark does give information about our Lord, and from this will come the springboard for conversation to put it all together.

Now here are some books on how to start and lead an evangelistic Bible study class. First, there's *How to Start a Neighborhood Bible Study* by Marilyn Kunz and Catherine Schell (Tyndale). Then there's *It's Alive* by Gladys Hunt (Harold Shaw). Inter-Varsity Press, Harold Shaw Publishers and Tyndale Press all offer a whole series of study discussion guides on Bible books as well as topical studies. They all have been tried and tested and found most effective.

Many more people could engage in this kind of Bible study leadership if only they had the proper tools. Some years ago, my wife Marie started a women's group and later we had several couples' groups in the evenings. Since then a good number of home studies have sprung up, all led by people who, like us, felt very timid at first. They said, "Oh, not me, I couldn't do it! I don't have a college or seminary education," etc., etc. But they put their eyes on the Lord rather than the difficulties. Their sheer enthusiasm about the Word of God and the benefits of small group study spurred them on. We all found there was a deep spiritual hunger in people from many diverse backgrounds. These friends responded easily to a no-strings-attached invitation to learn what the Bible is all about. It's been a most encouraging development to watch.

The Gold Mine of Clubs

Much of the question of church outreach revolves around children's clubs. The big challenge is to get people who are already interested in these clubs to participate in the general church fellowship. We make all kinds of contacts with young people in clubs, but many of their families never identify with our local churches. This outreach requires a vigorous visitation program to the parents. To me it's amazing the number of churches that have booming club programs but never get to the parents of the kids in those classes.

Our usual practice is to go banging from door to door for church visitation at random. All the while we actually have a gold mine waiting for us in the parents of the young people! But it takes a systematic program to get the job done. When parents know we are interested in their kids, we've touched a tender chord and they're more likely to be open to the gospel. Then it would be natural for them to identify with the fellowship of the local church.

Exploring New Ideas

Christian films can also be used, of course, and if you advertise widely, all kinds of people will respond. Show a Moody Science film or some other production in someone's basement for a starter. Invite new friends and make sure you provide the personal touch of friendship. Don't depend on an electric medium to do the whole job of winning people. At the end of each showing, conduct an open discussion on some point of the film.

Explore new ideas. Hold seminars on subjects that relate to the people's needs: forums on family living, marriage enrichment, budgeting principles for the Christian, challenges to adolescents in the seventies, an apologetic presentation of the Christian faith.

This last suggestion would be suited for the more intellectual or doctrinal needs of an audience. A good format is to have someone present the basic Christian tenets and then open the floor for questions and discussion. We did this in a church and found the response gratifying. For six months preceding the series, the Christians concentrated on getting to know new friends with the view to inviting them to the special meetings.

Realizing that non-churched people might not be familiar with our hymns and would perhaps feel more comfortable in a kind of academic atmosphere, we advertised a "lecture series" rather than a "church service." After each lecture, there were coffee klatches in homes where the discussions continued. I was told that more new people attended that series of four Friday night lectures than had attended any traditional evangelistic meetings in the church for 15 years.

Punt and Run?

Now let me say a word about tough areas. We've got to come to terms with this because some of our churches border on these areas and also because they are a part of the world for which our Lord is concerned. We can't say, for example, that we're not going to the Muslim areas of the world just because they're tough and unresponsive. We go there because the Lord has sent us. It seems somewhat incongruous to me that we spend thousands of dollars to send missionaries to black Africa but do very little to reach thirty million black Americans right here in our own country! The same could be said about any of the other minority groups. We stubbornly resist bridging the gap between us.

How can we, you and I, remedy the situation? We can't just punt and run, make one token attempt and give up. Let me suggest one way. Take initiative to get to know one person from a racial background different from your own, preferably a believer to begin with. If there are other races or ethnic groups within your own church, reach out to them personally, spend time with them. If your church does not have any of these, seek them out from another church in your community.

I was so convicted about this problem in my own life that I called a man I had heard about in one of the inner city black churches. I asked if it would be permissible for me and my family to come and visit his church. He seemed a little startled at first and asked, "Oh, would you like to speak?" I told him I would just like to come and join his people in their worship service. I think he was flabbergasted because in the past white men had visited them only when they were asked to speak. In fact, at that time black ministers were rarely invited to speak in white churches. (This fact was not lost on the black brethren, believe me.)

We went to their church several times and got to know them. Later they did invite me to speak. We went to one home for dinner and later invited them to ours. The fellowship was great and our children, theirs and ours, enjoyed each other. We got insights into their circumstances and saw struggles we had never dreamed of. We saw the difficulties of witnessing in a poor neighborhood, the problems the children have in getting a quality education, and the frequent threats of violence to their young people from street gangs. The first man I called was a senior biologist at the University of Chicago Medical School, his wife was a head nurse in the hospital. They continued to live in the downtown area in order to establish a strong witness there.

The Couple's Club at our church invited a group from that church of their own age to a potluck supper and a discussion of mutual concerns. It was enormously profitable. The general reaction was, "This is the first time I have met with someone from another race as a peer. It makes all the difference in the world in my attitudes." Prejudices were broken down on both sides. Each group was able to see and comprehend something of the love of Jesus Christ in the others.

If we take initiative as Christian groups and as individuals, we can make a contribution that will uniquely help to relieve racial tension and promote understanding. In the process we will learn how we as believers, who are one in Jesus Christ, can serve Him together.

Let me suggest two books: Tom Skinner's *Black and Free* (Zondervan) and Bill Pannell's book *My Friend, the Enemy* (Word). These books together opened my eyes to understand some of the feelings and problems of our black brethren today.

"You Do It First!"

Let me make one other suggestion in terms of church outreach; try to plan something in which church leaders and older people take the lead to go out into "enemy territory," so that the young people can see you in action. If all we're sayiing is they ought to go out and evangelize, but they never see *us* in action, we're not going to get very far.

A few years ago I preached in a church all summer at Belmar, New Jersey, while I was doing doctoral work at New York University. We got a vision of reaching out to some of the thousands of young people who congregated on the boardwalk and beach just two blocks from the church. So I said, "Look, let's go down there Saturday or Sunday night, give out some literature, and see if we can start some conversations." Well, my twelve-year-old son Paul was all excited about going with us. "Great, fine," I told him. "There will be kids your age there too. You can give them tracts." But he looked at me a little dubious, "No, that's O.K., Dad, I want to see how *you* do it first!"

Well, he spoke a profound truth. Let me put my money where my mouth is, as they say. After he saw me in action three or four times and got the feel of how to do it, he said, "Okay, there are some kids. I'll go give them some tracts."

"Dad, I want to see how you do it" is what some of our young people are saying to us as parents and as church leaders. Unless they see us in a role other than a formal one at church, I don't think we're really going to have much of an impact on them! They must see us in action. This will be worth 22 lectures. It's true that we need lectures and practical instruction, but we need the example as well. Like the old saying, "Your life speaks so loudly I can't hear what you're saying." To get dynamic results, it's your life—not just your lips—that must speak the powerful truth about Jesus Christ.

8

GOD'S WORD AND GIVING AWAY YOUR LIFE

"Icing on the cake" is what the average Christian's attitude seems to be toward using the Word of God, a kind of hobby for those who want to go all out and make Bible study a special interest. But for the run-of-the-mill person, let the professionals get into it. Does this sound familiar?

Imagine a young man receiving a daily letter from his girl friend. You would expect him to rush to a quiet place, tear it open and devour every word. Then he would mull over each part, envision the one who wrote it and go into a reverie about what her heart was saying to his heart. On the other hand, we would know there was something radically wrong if he decided to let each day's letter pile up until he had more time—perhaps Sunday afternoon, and then read the week's supply all at once. Almost by default, this is what we do with God's letter to us.

Now, think back to the man Jeremiah, in the Old Testament, who said he literally devoured God's word or "ate it up." As he ate, those very words became the joy and the delight of his heart (Jeremiah 15:16). In a similar attitude, Job "esteemed God's word more than his necessary food" (23:12). The Bible is God's letter to us. It's entire contents are for our instruction and learning. The whole purpose of its every page is for our benefit. It follows then that involvement with it is not optional equipment for those who care to take the trouble.

The glory of being a Christian and a servant of Jesus Christ is, among other things, that we have been given the true word that has come from God. We don't just have the collective wisdom of the ages; we have a word that has come from beyond, from the Creator. When you and I talk to others about the Christian faith, we don't have to say, "I think" or "the last vote we took seems to indicate thus and so" or "the trend is this way." And we don't have to tell people, "It's my idea against your idea." We can say, "Thus says the Lord."

The Real Argument

It's extremely important in witnessing that we never make it a contest. "That's what you think, but I think something else." If the discussion or controversy is between what *I* think and what *they* think, well, forget it. Their ideas will average out as good as mine. But their disagreement, if I'm faithfully communicating the Word of God, is with the *Lord Jesus Christ*, and not with me personally. If they want to argue with Him, O.K., but I want to be sure they know with whom they are arguing. It's not with me!

I have a friend who frequently speaks on college campuses. He often says with a twinkle in his eye, to somebody who is arguing some point, "Who do you think is a greater authority on that, you or Jesus Christ?" The person will gulp and say, "Well, I guess Jesus Christ." And my friend says, "Yeah, that's exactly right. Let me show you what He said." Boom. Very often this effectively makes the point: it's not just a question of *somebody else's* ideas contrasted to *ours*; it is the Word of God.

The Multifaceted Word

The Word of God is a fascinating thing because it has

such variety to it. For example, the Word of God is a hammer which breaks a rock in pieces. We all know how it has been used by the Spirit of God to break open and change someone whose thinking is like granite. The Word of God is also food; we're spiritually hungry and thirsty, so we come to the Word and find that it's milk and meat and encouragement. We've seen this in Jeremiah and Job. God's Word is spiritually refreshing to the drooping heart. It's also a guide and a lamp.

The entire world today is in need of some direction. Well, there is help! "Thy word is a lamp to my feet and a light to my path" (Psalm 119:105). The one sure thing we've got today amid all the phenomenal change around us is the Word of God. It remains the same. In its pages we find a fixed reference point when everything else is changing.

The Word is also water. Washing in it cleanses us. It was Dawson Trotman who said, "Sin will keep you from the Word of God and the Word of God will keep you from sin." The Word is fire too. Its heat will purge out impurities. It's also a sword, distinguishing between the thoughts of the flesh and of the Spirit (Hebrews 4:12). It's many more things too—in fact the most wonderful possession we have.

Taking the Word for Granted

One of the things we take for granted is that we have this Book in a language we can understand. All over the world today there are countries where the word of God is not available for personal use, yet we let it sit on our shelves and collect dust! Imagine the situation of the Christians in China. The Far Eastern Broadcasting Company in Hong Kong has developed a program to read the Word of God over the radio at dictation speed so people in remote parts of China can write it down. Letters from China show that this is the only way many people have access to the Bible. In contrast, you and I have the Word available to us in scores of versions!

Since we *have* the Word of God, how do we effectively study it? Biblical knowledge doesn't come by osmosis. This statement might seem to be a stranglehold on the obvious, but it constantly astounds me that there are people who think there must be some secret formula, some little pill or pamphlet that will make them an enlightened Bible student overnight. It just does not happen that way.

Taking In and Giving Out

People have come to my father and said, "Oh, my, I'd love to know what you know." He would reply, "It's really very simple; study the Word of God every day for fifty years!" There are no shortcuts. It's got to be done on a day-to-day basis, and it takes effort. It comes by diligent study, and it must be *personal* study.

Those of us who have had formal Bible classes will know that, as helpful as Bible school and seminary may be, unless we learn to study the Word of God for ourselves, we don't retain very much of what we've heard. We just don't assimilate very much of what other people digest for us. There is no substitute for study of the Word for ourselves if we really want to know it.

Somehow we've got to get ourselves in a position where we are forced to teach what we have studied. Then we will really remember it! I've been teaching in a seminary for several years. I've never grown so much in my life as I have by facing a class day after day after day. The best way to learn is to teach! The same thing will happen to us if we teach a Sunday school class or any other group. This is the way learning comes. What is taken in, must be given out.

Knowledge Without Formal Classes

Furthermore, it is not imperative to have a formal education. Again, if I may use my father as an illustration, all the formal education he ever had was one year at night school in the old Philadelphia School of the Bible, around 1915. Before that he had only *eight years* of formal education in a school for fatherless boys. (My grandfather died when Dad was four years old). My father graduated at the top of his class in 1913, was converted two years later, studied one year at night at PSOB and got the rest of his knowledge from his own personal study. Everything he ever gave from a conference platform or on the radio came as a result of diligent personal study. Few people (even with all kinds of degrees) knew the Word of God better than my father did. It's a matter of whether we are primarily willing to apply ourselves to Scripture, and then apply Scripture to ourselves.

Nothing Mysterious

Now there's really nothing mysterious about studying the Word of God. Somehow or other when it comes to spiritual things we tend to put them on a separate shelf or in a separate category, as if there's something different about them. How do we study anything? How do we learn to make out our income tax? Well, we read the instructions, and reread them, and then we try to figure out all the things we don't understand. We ask people we trust what a particular thing means, and we really work it over.

How do we study economics or physics? How did we study a subject in school? The same way. First we read it. Then reread it. Very, very simple. There's nothing profound, nothing magic about it. We just work at it. If we discover words we don't understand, what do we do? We look them up in the dictionary to find out what they mean. Amazingly profound, isn't it? Then we note questions that arise as we read the material. If we don't understand a concept, we get further help with it.

When we're getting ready to take an exam, we read the material, we underline it, we outline it, and finally we get to the place where we can close the book and think through what we've studied. This is the value of effective study. After we've read the material we retain something of what we have read, and if we have questions we get further help.

No Great Difference

The amazing thing is that this is really not too different from studying the Word of God. It's the same process. If we have questions, we go to a commentary to see what others have thought about the passage in question. We ask older Christians what their understanding of the passage is and pretty soon the whole thing begins to unfold for us.

Undoubtedly it's true that the Bible is different in one or two respects from other kinds of study. To begin with, we have the Holy Spirit to enlighten us about His Word. However, we have misinterpreted that statement by our Lord that says we have no need that anyone should teach us, that the Holy Spirit will enlighten us directly. This doesn't mean that we don't have to expose ourselves to the Word of God or to go through the process of study. The Holy Spirit illumines us *as we study*. We don't just go out under a banyan tree and meditate like a Hindu or a Buddhist, and then suddenly come up with a great flash of knowledge of the Word of God that floats down to us ethereally from beyond. No, the Holy Spirit illumines the Word that He has inspired, and He does this as we expose ourselves to it and study it.

No Mere Academics

The other difference between the Scriptures and any other book is that this Book is never to be studied from a merely academic point of view. This Book brings us into vital contact with the living God, and action is demanded of us on the basis of what we study.

The well-known author-preacher, Dr. D. Martyn Lloyd-Jones is vehemently opposed to the study of Scripture in any formal schooling sense. The idea of Bible school or seminary worries him. He contends that the Bible should never be studied academically, because it is always a spiritually living thing.

I don't completely agree with him, but he does make an important point. If Bible study ever becomes purely academic, then the Freudian slip, "What cemetery did you go to?" may well become true of us. The Word of God is breathed into us by the Spirit of God, and we're not just studying words to master an outline so we can pass an examination. We're studying in order to respond to the living God who has inspired it. And after we respond to His Word we are able to communicate it to others for a spiritual purpose.

Sawdust in Our Mouths?

If we don't apply God's Word to ourselves in a personal way, we may find that our study becomes sawdust in our mouths—worse than useless. This is an easy trap to fall into. We need to say continually, as the hymn says, "Beyond the sacred page we seek *Thee*, Lord." Here is where we find the unfolding of the character and personality of the living God Himself.

Remember the Pharisees; they were great at knowing the Word of God. They could stick pins in the scroll of Scripture and quote any verse the pin would go through! They knew it so well that our Lord said in John 5:39, 40, "You search the Scriptures, because you think that *in them* you have eternal life; and it is they that bear witness to *me*." It's possible to get too involved with the mechanism of the telescope as such. But the purpose of the telescope is to see the stars. The same way the Bible is for getting into the presence of God.

What Does It Say?

Now how do we actually go about this kind of Bible study? We should interact with three basic questions. These are useful for personal study as well as for preparing to lead a group Bible study discussion.

Question one is, "What does it say?" Outline the paragraph. Even with a well known passage you'll get some new insights. Ask questions such as, Who is it talking about? What is happening? Where? When? How? Just factual questions; list these facts. These are questions that involve observation.

You'd be amazed at the number of people who leap into deciding what the Bible means before they have honestly read it to see what it actually says. It's always a jolt to us to scrutinize for ourselves what a Bible text says and discover it is completely different than we thought it was. Our information may have come to us secondhand fifteen years before.

What Dr. So-and-So has said isn't the final word; the final word is what the Word of God itself says. One good way to study the Word of God is to say to yourself, "Suppose I had never read this before in my life." Try this with something as familiar as John 3:16. Then take the three questions and work through them personally, and I'll guarantee that you'll get something fresh out of it—something you've never thought of before.

What Does It Mean?

Question two is, "What does it mean?" It's one thing to see what the text *says*; it's another thing to understand what it *means*. Now this is probably the most difficult phase and where we are likely to get hung up. This is the science of hermeneutics, which is simply the science of interpretation.

"Oh," you say, "I don't need anything like that. The Bible is transparently clear. I take it literally, and that's that."

But is it that simple? Do we always take every statement literally? The answer to that question is pivotal. When Psalm 114:4 says, "The mountains skipped like rams" and Isaiah 55:12 says, "The trees of the field shall clap their hands," does this mean that we can go out this afternoon and look for the mountains that go leaping around, and that we can cup our ears to hear the applause of the trees? Well, of course we don't mean that.

The Ten Commandments say, "Honor your father and your mother." This is reaffirmed in Ephesians as the only commandment with promise. Yet the Gospels record that our Lord said, "Unless a man hate his father and mother he cannot be my disciple." Now which is it? We can't have it both ways. We're forced into hermeneutics whether we like it or not. It's the question of how we understand and interpret each part of the Word of God in its context. We must come to terms with this issue. If we don't we'll get into all kinds of wild aberrations.

Literal Versus Figurative

What is it to take the Bible literally? When someone asks me that question on a university campus I answer, "I take the Bible literally in the sense that it was intended by the writer for the people to whom it was written." This means that when the writer intended to express himself in figurative language (as David obviously did in some of the Psalms), I understand that this is figurative. On the other hand, when he intended it to be literal, I take it to be literal.

We certainly don't interpret everything "spiritually," which is what the Christian Scientists and some other groups do in an attempt to explain away the miracles of the Bible. We can't read the text of the Bible without realizing that the writer intended those miracles to be accepted at face value by the reader. Yet in other cases it's obvious that figures of speech are being used.

It's really not all that difficult. There are figures of speech used in our newspapers every day. As you read these you don't need a college education to know that these are figures of speech (for example, expressions used in an account of a ballgame or a description of a news event). We understand inductively when they are being used. We know that "Johnny Bench hit a shot over the left field wall" doesn't mean he stood with a rifle on home plate shooting over the left field wall! We know that this is a figure of speech describing a solid line drive into the bleachers! We use and understand the rudiments of hermeneutics every day.

Honest Difference of Opinion

Let me add this about Bible interpretation. *My understanding* of what the Word of God says in a particular passage is distinct from the *Word of God itself.* There is, in many passages, room for honest difference of opinion among equally committed believers as to what the Bible is saying. I must never say about one of these disputed passages, "If you don't agree with me, you're not subject to the Word of God." How many times have I heard this said, and how many churches have been blown apart because somebody has taken such a know-it-all position!

This is a far different thing from agreeing unanimously on what the message of a particular passage is saying and then having somebody object, "But I cannot accept that." That's where you're over the hill of orthodoxy. There may be honest differences of opinion on the interpretation of a given passage, but when we agree as to what the Bible is actually teaching, then we must submit ourselves to it as the final supreme court. It is the authoritative Word of God; we bow to it.

Rejecting the Teaching

Can you distinguish between a difference of interpretation and an unwillingness to accept what we agree the passage is saying? Some years ago a very prominent scholar was in our home in New York. He was a brilliant atomic chemist and he also had a Ph.D. in philosophy of religion. He was a real believer and was gifted in evangelism, but he had a neo-orthodox view of Scripture. When we got on the question of a historic Adam, we went round and round on the thing, and I kept saying, "Gil, if I didn't have the fifth chapter of Romans to contend with stating there is a historic Adam, there would be many different possibilities of interpretation of Genesis 1 to 3. But if Romans five in the Greek language means anything at all, you can't get away from the fact that Paul believed in a historic Adam. The whole of Paul's argument was based on a historic Adam, including Christ as the Second Adam."

Finally, after about three hours, it became sort of like Indian wrestling—back and forth. Finally he threw up his hands and said, "Well, all right, Paul obviously believed in a historic Adam—he believed the rabbinic tradition of his time—but Paul was wrong!" "Well," I said, "O.K. That's a far different thing from saying that that's not what the Bible is saying." If you agree on what the Bible teaches, but you don't *accept* what it teaches, these are two completely different issues.

Hermeneutics is essentially the basic method by which we interpret Scripture. We don't have space to cover it thoroughly in this chapter, but let me suggest a couple of books for you. If you're really interested in following this through, you'll find that it's really worth the study. In my judgment the best book on hermeneutics is *Interpreting the Bible* by A. Berkeley Mickelsen (Eerdmans). Another excellent book is *Protestant Biblical Interpretation* by Bernard Ramm (Baker).

What Does It Mean to Me?

Now here's the most crucial question of all: "What does the Bible mean to me personally?" *Observation* is important ("What does it say?"). So is interpretation ("What does it mean?"). But the goal is to answer the question "*So what?*" ("What does it mean to *me*?").

Unless we understand the personal application of Scripture, we have missed the whole point. Even so-called abstract doctrinal truths have tremendous practical applications. Take justification by faith, for example. What does this mean to me today? Well, if I stop and meditate about it, I realize that it has tremendous implications for my attitude toward life. If I get the truth of justification by faith down into the warp and woof of my life, it will affect all of my living. But unfortunately, we don't always take the time to really drive the results of our Bible study and teaching down into the practical areas of our lives.

The Tools of Study

What are some of the tools we can use to get these good things out of Scripture? Well, there are of course various versions of the Scriptures. Which is the best version? We can't be positively sure till we get to heaven, but here are some suggestions. The King James is still in wide use, though in the judgment of most scholars it is not the most accurate version by any means. It has some hard-to-understand Elizabethan terms. But let's keep in touch with it, since many people still use it regularly.

I'll never forget how I was persuaded of the value of modern English versions. When I was at American Keswick some years ago, a Buddhist Thai student was rooming with me, and he had bought a beautiful gold-leaf, leatherbound King James reference Bible. Wonderful. Great. The only thing is, he never read it! The fact is, he simply couldn't figure it out. When I came back from breakfast (he had slept in) he was propped up in bed with my little 75-cent paperback RSV (Revised Standard Version) New Testament that I had left on my bureau. He was reading through the Gospel of John, and he was already up to chapter 6. His eyes were like saucers as he said, "I understand!" He could read and understand it because it was written in contemporary English.

Use Several Versions

The Revised Standard Version does raise some questions, so I suggest that we have several versions and compare them. Also, there is a difference between a translation and a paraphrase. *The Living Bible* is extremely popular now, and I must confess I'm very slow to knock it when I've seen my own teenage daughter reading it like mad every day. It clearly communicates. *The Living Bible* is a *paraphrase* containing some interpretation. As a basic study version I think the *New American Standard Bible* is considered to be one of the most accurate, and the *New International Version* is excellent. Our interpretive problems often clear up as we compare various translations. If there's still doubt about the meaning, go to a reliable commentary for further help.

A Good Concordance

A good concordance is of first rate value. Learn to look up meanings of words and see how they are used in different ways throughout the Bible. Not all words are used in exactly the same way all through Scripture. For instance, Paul used the word "flesh" in seven different ways even though it is uniformly translated from the one Greek word "sarx." If I'm not aware of these differences I'm going to get gummed up as I impose my own uniform meaning on the word all through Scripture.

It's not essential to know Greek or Hebrew. But I would suggest a *Strong's Concordance*. As you look up the English word in Strong's, it shows the various Hebrew and Greek words that are translated as one English word. Different shades of meaning are given that you might not have considered. To use the above illustration of "flesh," the word might refer to the physical part of the body, the living person as a whole, all living creatures both man and animals, the natural being that comes from inheritance as opposed to divine regeneration, or that element in man's nature that is opposed to goodness and makes him evil. That's only a starter to tease you into further curiosity! Strong's will also help locate particular references for you. It's obvious I feel it is an indispensable volume. Of course, it will take time to use but the rewards will make it completely worthwhile.

Remember that the original words of Scripture are God-breathed. If we believe that Scripture came from the mind of God through the Holy Spirit, then we evangelical believers should be knowledgeable about the exact meaning the text implies as it comes to us from the Hebrew and Greek.

More Good Books

Another asset is a good Bible dictionary. The best one-volume work I know of is *The New Bible Dictionary*, published by Eerdmans. We also need a good commentary. Begin with a good one-volume work that will take you through the whole Bible. Try the one by Jamieson, Fausset and Brown (Zondervan), *The New Bible Commentary* (Eerdmans), or the *Wycliffe Bible Commentary* by Moody Press. But whichever one you use, be *sure* that you study the Bible *first*, and then look at the commentary. Don't read the commentary first and then study the Bible. Nobody has a monopoly on all the truth of God, and we should be very sure we test everything by the Word of God itself, not by what some particular person says.

How can we study? Well, we can study either book-by-book or topically. As we lay out a program it's amazing how we begin to get a grip on the Word of God. One very useful self-study aid is *This Morning with God*, a four-volume set by Inter-Varsity Press. The format is based solely on questions to elucidate the text. It will take you through the whole Bible in five years if you're willing to put a half-hour a day into it.

In Your Regular Schedule

One last thing. Nothing we've said in this chapter will be of any profit to us unless we sit down with our schedules and decide when we are going to study the Bible. If we wait until we find time for it, we'll end up never studying the Bible at all; it's that simple. People ask me, "Where do you find the time to do this, that, or the other thing?" I don't find time to do anything. I *take* time to do it. This may mean I can't take time to do certain other things.

All of us have twenty-four hours a day—no more, no less. We're all equal in that way. I must decide what is really important, and take the time to put it into my schedule. It's unlikely that any of us will study the Bible regularly unless we establish a given period of time on a daily basis, plus a longer period of time on, say one evening each week or on the weekend. Then, as we devote ourselves to the study of the Word of God, it's in our schedules. When other things come up that could take us away from it, we can say, "Sorry, I'm booked. I've got an appointment." And thus keep our appointment with God to study His Word.

When we have done this for a while we will begin to realize that we are beginning to absorb the Word of God as the Spirit of God illumines it. We'll have a tool by which we can help other people. Our own faith will be strengthened as well. All the spiritual profit that comes with Bible study will be ours forever. But it won't happen by just thinking it's a great idea. It will happen by our digging into it consistently so we can give it away along with our lives.

9

THE GREAT ANTICIPATION FOR THE FUTURE IN GIVING AWAY YOUR LIFE

In the dead of winter, when the peaks of the Rocky mountains are blanketed with snow, silent and seemingly unpeopled, our family regularly edged up the winding Stage Road of Cheyenne mountain just south of Colorado Springs. At the very top of the 9000 foot mountain, cratered in a small hollow, is Bear Trap Ranch where college students gather for holiday conferences. At Thanksgiving, Christmas and Easter, the Ranch is largely attended by international students from schools all over the country.

I am always astounded at the quality of the students who come. They represent every field of study, every strata of their societies and many countries of the world. Parenthetically, if you are in a college or university community where God has literally brought the world to your doorstep, don't overlook your opportunity to share Christ with them. You can be a missionary in your own language and in your own living room if you are willing to reach out in friendship to them. They may never hear the gospel in their own countries and if one of them goes home a believer, he or she will be worth five missionaries.

Several years ago at Bear Trap, as we were presenting the

basics of Christianity to the students we got onto the subject of the second coming of Christ. This fascinated a Muslim student from Damascus, Syria, who came to me after the meeting and said, "Did I understand you to say that Jesus Christ is coming again?" I replied, "Yes, that's right; He is coming again." And I added, "That's my only hope for peace. That's my only hope for any solution to the international tensions." The student responded, "You really believe He's coming again?" Again, I told him, "I'm certain that He is coming again. And that is our great hope." The Muslim student then looked me in the eye and said, "Those are the most comforting words I have heard in a long time."

The future coming again of our Lord Jesus Christ is the greatest anticipation in life for the Christian. Sometimes I wonder if we shouldn't emphasize the second coming as part of the gospel more than we do since it is the culmination of the Biblical message to us. The gospel is incomplete without it.

The promise of our Lord's coming is very clear. For example, our Lord said in those wonderful words of John 14:1-3, "Let not your hearts be troubled; believe in God, believe also in me. In my Father's house are many rooms; if it were not so, would I have told you that I go to prepare a place for you, I will come again and will take you to myself, that where I am you may be also." Remember it was our Lord Himself who said to the disciples and to each of us, "I am going away to prepare a place for you, but I will come again." We have His word for it. We take His word in salvation, and we say that the way we know we're saved is not by how we feel but by the fact that *the Lord Jesus Christ Himself has said it.* We also take Him at His word concerning His second coming to earth.

The Words of Angels—and of Paul and Peter

Remember also the words of the angels when our Lord

had led His disciples outside the city of Jerusalem. He gave them the promise of the Holy Spirit and the commission to be witnesses everywhere. Then, "He was lifted up, and a cloud took him out of their sight. And while they were gazing into heaven as he went, behold, two men stood by them in white robes, and said, 'Men of Galilee, why do you stand looking into heaven? This Jesus, who was taken up from you into heaven, will come in the same way as you saw him go into heaven' " (Acts 1:9-11). So you see we have the word of the angels too.

And then we have that same message in 1 Thessalonians 4:16-18, where Paul says, by inspiration of the Holy Spirit, "For the Lord himself will descend from heaven with a cry of command, with the archangel's call, and with the sound of the trumpet of God. And the dead in Christ will rise first; then we who are alive, who are left, shall be caught up together with them in the clouds to meet the Lord in the air; and so we shall always be with the Lord. Therefore comfort one another with these words."

Likewise from Peter, we have these words: "But *the day of the Lord will come* like a thief, and then the heavens will pass away with a loud noise, and the elements will be dissolved with fire, and the earth and the works that are upon it will be burned up" (2 Peter 3:10).

The New Song

Then there's that magnificent passage in the Book of the Revelation, in which John gives us a prophetic insight into the last times. He begins by saying they sang a new song and "then I looked, and I heard around the throne and the living creatures and the elders the voice of many angels, numbering myriads of myriads and thousands of thousands, saying with a loud voice, 'Worthy is the Lamb who was slain, to receive power and wealth and wisdom and might and honor and glory and blessing!' And I heard every creature in heaven and on earth and under the earth and in the sea, and all therein, saying, 'To him who sits upon the throne and to the Lamb be blessing and honor and glory and might forever and ever!' " (Rev. 5:11-13).

When a great choir sings that anthem from the *Messiah* oratorio, "Worthy is the Lamb," it's a tremendous thing. Yet it's just a pale reflection of the great anthem and chorus of which we will all be a part in heaven. What are the implications of this great fact of the coming of the Lord Jesus Christ for us? What should it mean to you and me today? It means an abundance of good things for our day-by-day enjoyment.

The Blessed Hope

The first thing is what has been called "our blessed hope." The expectation of Christ's return gives us hope, the opposite of despair. Are you ever tempted to despair as you look all around you? When you see the political turmoil, the tensions wracking our society and the world, when you see the nuclear armaments proliferating and realize you are sitting on a powder keg, when you see evil triumphing in all kinds of places, are you ever tempted to despair?

As we remember continually that the Lord Jesus Christ is going to return and reign supreme, that He is going to be the King of Kings and Lord of Lords, we can and should be brought out of despair and into hope despite the darkness that may seem to encompass us and overwhelm us.

If your political candidate hasn't won his election, don't despair—the end has not yet come. If war breaks out again in the Middle East, don't despair—the end has not yet come. If more countries develop nuclear capability beyond what they have now, don't despair—the end has not yet come. Believe it or not, the Lord Jesus Christ is still in ultimate control of history. Sometimes we seem to be careening down a hill out of control, and the political leaders of the world, with all their enormous power, are unable to bring about a turn-around. Yet the world is not out of control. It is subject to God's long-range plan.

The Author of History

God, the Author of history, is going to bring it to a successful conclusion. The Lord Jesus Christ is going to return, and this is our great hope. This fact is what that Muslim student glimpsed as we talked about the coming again of Jesus Christ.

In one of his books, Helmut Thielicke of Germany makes a statement that has made a profound impact on me and has never left me. He observes, "When the drama of history is over, Jesus Christ will stand alone upon the stage, and every power figure of history—Alexander the Great, Charlemagne, Stalin, Mao Tse-tung, and anybody else you want to include—will realize that he has been only a bit actor in the drama put on by God. What a tremendous thing to grasp. At the end of history the Lord Jesus Christ will stand supreme, alone upon the stage as King of Kings and Lord of Lords. However powerful any political leader seems to be today, however powerful the forces of evil may seem to be, they are only transient.

What a tremendous comfort this must be to all our fellow believers who suffer oppression for their faith! And what a tremendous comfort it can be to us if we ever face a time when our society discriminates against believers. The possibility of oppression is not as unlikely as some of us might like to think. You and I may yet see persecution or the judgment of God in a way that Christians have in other countries. However strong any political tyranny may be, it's only temporary. Jesus Christ is the ultimate Ruler and the One who will ultimately triumph.

Incontestable Triumph of God's Son

The route to that triumph has not been an easy one for

our Lord Jesus. In his letter to the Philippians Paul speaks of our Lord's willingness to become obedient to the point of death on a cross. Then he describes the action of God the Father. It begins with "therefore," or because of Christ's obedience and suffering, God will recompense Him for the humiliation. "Therefore, God has highly exalted Him." He shall have a name above every other name. Every knee and every tongue in heaven and earth shall bow before Him, acknowledge Him as Lord to the glory of God the Father, Philippians 2:9. This will be when that magnificent chorus of worship will break forth. The incontestable triumph of God's son over all opposition infuses us with boundless courage and strength.

Most of us who are born again find ourselves in settings in which true believers are in the minority, and sometimes in a *despised* minority. Some of us may associate with some very sophisticated people who, though not attacking us directly, may with withering condescension look upon us as naive for believing in the supernatural, in Jesus Christ. And that hurts. It's hard. When we're overwhelmed and in the minority we sometimes wonder if we can wait.

King of Kings and Lord of Lords

At such times we can remind ourselves that the day is coming when Jesus Christ will declare Himself in history and will be known by all men as King of Kings and Lord of Lords. Your most supercilious professor will bow his knees to Jesus. Your mocking neighbor will come to recognize Christ as the Ruler of the universe, unless by the grace of God he receives Christ before that time. Whoever it is that gives you a hard time for your faith, in that day, will recognize the truth which he despised while here on earth. The time is coming when you and I personally, as well as our Lord Jesus Christ, will be vindicated. Every knee will bow, and every tongue confess, that Jesus Christ is Lord.

You and I are on the winning side. It may not seem so in a given instance, when we are by ourselves or greatly outnumbered, but we need to keep the long view in mind. We can take courage, not in a vindictive sense—"You'll get yours!"—none of that at all, but with an aching heart and the realization that the time is coming when every person will recognize that Jesus Christ is Lord, to the glory of God the Father.

Does this give you courage as you contemplate it? It should. It should grip us all each day as we go out to face that world to which God has sent us.

Relief from Anxiety

The coming again of the Lord Jesus Christ should also give us certainty and assurance—relief from anxiety for the future. Paul was gripped by the bright outlook ahead. He wrote to the church at Philippi, "I am sure that he who began a good work in you will bring it to completion at the day of Jesus Christ" (Philippians 1:6). God is at work in you and me to accomplish His good pleasure. Though we fail, He never fails; He is going to bring His work to a successful conclusion. As Paul also wrote, "He is able to guard me until that Day which has been entrusted to me."

There isn't much in this world that you and I can be sure of. We can't always be sure of friendship. We certainly can't be sure of political, social, or personal security; we can't be sure of economic security; we can't be sure of physical health. But of one thing we *can* be absolutely sure, the unchangeableness of our Lord Jesus Christ and the absolute certainty of His work in and through us. That's why we can know that He is going to bring that work to a glorious conclusion.

It is a great comfort to me to know that the Lord Jesus Christ is not finished with His work in me. I hope it's a comfort to you, too. We're all desperately aware of our infirmities and our failings, but we have the confidence that

God is at work in us to do His own good pleasure. He is going to bring His work to fruition so that in the great coming day we will be like Him.

He will come whether any of us believe it now or not. But why not believe it and thereby enjoy the day-by-day peace that its reality can give us?

We Sorrow Not as Others

The teaching of 1 Thessalonians 4:13-18 is that we are going to be with the Lord forever. We'll be reunited with those who have gone on before. Therefore "we sorrow not as others, who have no hope."

It's not that there's no sorrow at all. Some people would give the impression that if a Christian sheds a tear at the death of a loved one, somehow that's weakness. My brother-in-law dropped dead with a heart attack several years ago, and my sister had five children. He was a wonderful Christian, too. I had never really understood the meaning of the shortest verse in the Bible, "Jesus wept," until that time. I was gratified to remember that our Lord wept at the tomb of Lazarus; He was not dry-eyed about human sorrow.

But we do not sorrow as though we had no hope. We are comforted by the fact that "to be absent from the body is to be present with the Lord." We are not desolated by death, because for us death has become a servant to take us to Christ. Jesus Christ is coming again and is going to raise those who have gone before, and He will take those who are yet alive on earth to be with Him forever. We can take comfort in that fact. Though we recognize the sorrow that is in death, we also know that each person who goes on to the other side makes it that much more attractive, and of course the Son Himself is the greatest attraction of all.

Stimulus to Service

Another important implication of the coming of the Lord Jesus Christ that should grip us as we wait for Him is that His coming is a great stimulus to work. In 1 John 2:28 the writer says, "Now, little children, abide in him, so that when he appears we may have confidence and not shrink from him in shame at his coming."

How is it in your household when you know a visitor is coming? Sometimes there's tremendous pressure. Everybody's going crazy trying to get everything straightened up, and boy, in our house, we really hustle. I wish it could be that way in our Christian lives all the time. Have you ever known someone was coming to see you but didn't know exactly when? And you've felt really shaken out of your chair when they showed up without warning?

We had some relatives arrive unannounced from out of state one time, and I almost had a heart attack when I saw them walk in to stay with us for three days. We weren't prepared and I had a number of commitments. (I'm sure they did it out of kindness so we wouldn't go to a lot of work to prepare for them. Their motivation was good, I know.) But when we know someone is coming we make all kinds of preparations, don't we? From God's point of view, each one of us should be preparing for the return of Christ—we should be ready for His coming at any time. There may be changes and preparations we should make because our Lord Jesus Christ might come back this afternoon, or next week or anytime.

Do We Want Him Now?

Some of us aren't sure we want Him to come right now—we have things in mind that we want to do before He returns. Maybe there is a conversation we ought to have with someone with whom we've had a misunderstanding. Well, if we really believe in the second coming of our Lord, now is the time to get that straightened out, difficult though it may be. It may mean we must ask for forgiveness or seek to be forgiven.

Some of us have had in mind something we wanted to do for Jesus Christ but we have put it off for a more convenient time. We need to start working on it right now if we are going to be ready for Christ at His coming. There may be something we should stop doing because we know we'd be ashamed of it when He comes.

Then there are things we can do now that we won't be able to do in eternity. Now is our only opportunity to do them. The only opportunity to share our material substance in supporting the work of the Lord is in this life. Our only opportunity to witness to the lost is in this life. There are numbers of things for which our only opportunity is now, while we are waiting for His certain return.

Invest Today

One of the great subtleties that must come from the Enemy, because it can be so devastating, is the misconception that somehow a successful Christian life is some great amorphous blob out there in the future when we'll do some great exploit. Spiritual success for some of us always seems to be somewhere out in the future. The fact of the matter is that the depth and reality and quality of your Christian life and mine is measured exclusively by what it consists of *today*. It's what I invest for Jesus Christ now that will determine whether I'm serving Him and following Him tomorrow and the next day. It is not some great thing off in the future that gives us a successful Christian life. Life is merely an accumulation of days lived for Jesus Christ.

We can learn from John Wesley. When someone asked Wesley one morning, "What would you do if you knew the Lord were coming tonight?" he pulled out his appointment book and said, "Well, at ten o'clock I would be preparing a sermon for Springfield tonight, and at eleven o'clock I would be seeing Mr. So and So, and at twelve o'clock I would be having lunch, and at two o'clock I would be resting, and at three o'clock I would be stirring, and at four o'clock I would be leaving for Springfield." And he put his book back in his pocket!

Wesley so lived in the light of the reality of the coming of Jesus Christ that his life was ordered on a daily basis. He knew that time itself belongs to the Lord Jesus Christ. He was gripped by the reality of the second coming of our Lord, but this conviction worked itself out in the daily routine of his life. He tried to do all things for the glory of God. What a beautiful aim—waiting for our Lord Jesus Christ and His coming. This is the true stimulus to work and to devotion.

This great expectation for the future brings with it a desire for a pure life. 1 John 3:2, 3 says "Beloved, we are God's children now; it does not yet appear what we shall be, but we know that when He appears we shall be like Him for we shall see Him as He is. And everyone who thus hopes in Him purifies himself as He is pure." It does make a difference. It makes a difference in our goals and in our actions. And we do need to be purified daily.

This reminds me of a good friend. He is a highly successful surgeon and could live in a very elaborate life style. Instead, he gives his time and services generously to the Lord's work and to missions. He spends long periods overseas helping rural mission hospitals and gives his money generously to the Lord. We were talking about his need for a new car and someone suggested a Mercedes. His reply was, "That's not where I want to spend my money. Nor do I care about a flashy image. I am a servant of God and I want to look like one." He has his goals lined up with the coming of the Lord.

Driving on to the End

If we are truly conscious of His coming, we will persevere

in our Christian walk. The Apostle Paul drove on to the end. He hit the Christian life with the throttle wide open. He died with his boots on, and it was the certainty of the coming again of the Lord Jesus Christ that kept him in that attitude despite any calamity that came. The obstacles might have overwhelmed most other people but Paul kept going because he had his eyes fixed on the Lord. In 2 Timothy 4:6-8 he wrote, "I am already on the point of being sacrificed; the time of my departure has come. I have fought the good fight, I have finished the race, I have kept the faith. Henceforth there is laid up for me the crown of righteousness, which the Lord, the righteous judge, will award to me on that Day and not only to me but to all who have loved his appearing." That's persevering to the end!

If, on the other hand, the feeling comes, "I don't think I can go through another year, I feel like throwing in the sponge" and discouragement overwhelms, that's the tool of the Enemy. Fight him. Fight the feelings. Don't flake out and give up. Don't let the ship get wrecked.

The story of Nehemiah gives a graphic picture of the success in restoring the wall around the city of Jerusalem. The odds against the Israelites were great. The enemy was far stronger than they were. And the people were overwhelmingly discouraged.

There were two things Nehemiah told the people. The first was, "Remember the Lord God of Heaven who is great and keeps His covenant and steadfast love with those who keep His commandments." He knew God was greater than the enemy. He was unshaken in this conviction.

The second fact he told them was that they should not give up. He said, "Fight for your brethren, your sons, your daughters, your wives and your homes" (Nehemiah 4:14). He concluded, "Our God will fight for us." It was God's will for them to wage the warfare against the enemy, to aggressively trust the Lord and pray. God heard their prayers and the wall was built.

There *is* a daily fight in the Christian life, you know. Paul talked about fighting, wrestling and praying. It was only when he approached the end of his life that he said, "I have fought a good fight. I have kept going to the end. I haven't quit and I have kept the faith."

Take the Long View

Paul persevered to the end, and we too need to wait for the Lord Jesus Christ with our minds fixed on Him. Do you have the long view today? Have you been so absorbed with immediate matters, seeing so many huge trees looming right in front of your eyes, that you can't see the panorama of the great forest of what God is doing? Have you lost sight of the culmination of God's history and your personal involvement in it?

As you read these words, I wonder if you have caught a new glimpse of something that God might be willing to do through you when you give away your life to Him. I pray that your enthusiasm will not wane, but that it may be a fire set in your heart by the Holy Spirit Himself, who will keep it burning until your desire and your enthusiasm are translated into action for God's glory.